Socially Sustainable Cities

Principles and Practices

Antoine S. Bailly, Philippe Brun, Roderick J. Lawrence, Marie-Claire Rey eds.

Socially Sustainable Cities

Principles and Practices

Programme UNESCO-MOST
Management of Social Transformations

Canton of Geneva,
Département de l'aménagement, de l'équipement et du logement
(Department of Planning, Infrastructure and Housing)

D∩ΞL
Département de l'aménagement
de l'équipement et du logement

M⊙ST

UNESCO

UNIVERSITÉ DE GENÈVE

ΘΘ ECONOMICA
London • Paris • Genève

Published by Economica Ltd,
9 Wimpole Street
London W1M 8LB

© Economica Ltd, 2000

First published 2000

Printed in France

Antoine S. Bailly, Philippe Brun,
Roderick J. Lawrence, Marie-Claire Rey eds.

Socially Sustainable Cities

ISBN 1-902282-09-4

Acknowledgements

The texts were adapted, translated and edited by Marie-Claire Rey and Roderick Lawrence from the papers presented at the UNESCO-MOST Colloquiums in Geneva and Cape Town. The editorial team also included Antoine Bailly and Philippe Brun.

The editors wish to thank the *Département de l'aménagement, de l'équipement et du logement* of the Canton of Geneva for its support since 1995, particularly the Department Minister Laurent Moutinot and his predecessor Philippe Joye. They also thank Richard Anderegg and Claude Torche for their active participation in the project, as well as Judith Bell in Toronto, Canada who carried out the final editing of the English manuscript.

The editors thank the organisers of the Montreal-Toronto and Cape Town Colloquiums, Professor Mario Polèse of the *Institut National de la Recherche Scientifique-Urbanisation* in Montreal and Professor Richard Stren at the University of Toronto, as well as the Cape Metropolitan Council and Professor John Abbott at the University of Cape Town.

Finally, the editors gratefully acknowledge the support of UNESCO — and in particular Ali Kazancigil and Geneviève Domenach-Chich of the Social Science, Research and Policy Division — for its financial contribution to the Montreal-Toronto, Geneva and Cape Town Colloquiums as well as to the publication of this book.

Geneva

October 2000

Contents

List of figures

Sustainable urban development

A NETWORK FOR SOCIALLY SUSTAINABLE URBAN MANAGEMENT

Since 1995, eleven partner cities around the world have been involved in an international research project, *Towards Socially Sustainable Cities*, sponsored by the UNESCO Programme *Management of Social Transformations (MOST)* (see Chapter 1.1).

The research project aims at *"building an internationally comparable knowledge base for urban management, that is useful both for researchers and practitioners."* The emphasis has been on analysing urban policies from an international perspective and across sectors. The following objectives have been tabled:

- to concentrate on the analysis of key local policy areas;
- to integrate spatial planning and social perspectives;
- to compare urban policy experience and give concrete steps and guidelines to improve the social sustainability of cities.

Other programmes also tackle the present urban contradictions and look for better urban management solutions for the future: the programmes of the World Bank, of the United Nations (HABITAT), of the Mega-cities Conference. They use the expertise of various scientific fields, such as architecture, geography, and sociology. In each case, the central issue is finding solutions for social urban development and policies to be implemented. However only a few of these programmes are specifically geared towards local policies. The objective of the UNESCO/MOST project is to compare metropolitan policies and their local impacts.

1.1   UNESCO-MOST Research Project on the Sustainability of Cities

"MOST is a research programme, designed by UNESCO, to promote international comparative social science research. Its primary emphasis is to support large-scale, long- term autonomous research and to transfer the relevant findings and data to decision-makers." (For further information, consult UNESCO homepage: http://www.unesco.org/most)

One of the MOST research themes is *Cities as arenas of accelerated social transformations.* In 1995, a research project was launched under this theme to consider social and spatial policies that promote sustainable urban management. The partner cities in this project have included Baltimore, Budapest, Cape Town, Geneva, Lyon, Miami, Montreal, Nairobi, San Salvador, São Paulo, Toronto and Utrecht. The teams bring together academics and, in certain cases, civil servants and policy makers.

The initial meeting was held in Montreal and Toronto in 1995, and was followed by a colloquium in Geneva in 1996. A third meeting was organised in Cape Town inSeptember 1998.

A first volume of studies from the MOST Network is entitled *The Social Sustainability of Cities: Diversity and the Management of Change* (Polèse and Stren, 2000).

An asset of the MOST project is its focus on a neglected aspect of urban management: the social dimension. The emphasis of planning policies has been for the most part on land-use and urban form. Similarly, the social dimension of sustainability has rarely been in the foreground or considered with an attention equal to that given to the environmental and economic perspectives.

The specificity of the MOST project lies also in its composition and its practical dimension. This group of people, which brings together varied representatives of the academic world, policy-makers and politicians, provides a platform for an open and interdisciplinary debate on urban management practices.

This publication compile the main issues selected for discussion at the MOST Colloquiums held in Geneva and in Cape Town. The book consists of introductory chapters on six urban management themes, illustrated by social policy examples presented at the colloquiums. The conference papers (listed in Appendix) have been summarised and adapted with the approval of the authors.

Photo: Cape Metropolitan Council

Figure 1.1 **When the City Spreads Chaotically:** *informal settlements in Cape Town*

SUSTAINABILITY FOR URBAN QUALITY OF LIFE

Urban growth and metropolisation are two key processes of the 20th century that will also characterise the 21st century. These trends could be considered as positive to the extent that they improve the quality of life of city dwellers. However, they also bring about a series of urban planning, economic and social problems. Even without clear statistical data, the scars of poverty in cities in both developed and so called "developing countries" are obvious: the deprived groups in urban areas of the South are estimated to represent more than 40% of the population. Cities in industrial countries are confronted by a similar social turmoil, with their neighbourhoods of exclusion, homelessness, vandalism, unrest and drug abuse, etc.

A number of these problems are linked to the economic situation in cities abandoned by private enterprises looking for comparative advantage, or submerged by fast-growing immigration.

However, with the empowerment of urban local authorities, cities are becoming key stakeholders, able to reverse these tendencies or to bring solutions. Surely, not everything desirable, sustainable and possible can be achieved; but without urban development control, the city spreads chaotically, and lacks coherent infrastructure or service provision. This opens the way to ghettos, illegal settlements, insecurity, organised crime, and illegal employment, etc. There are numerous examples: cities like Lagos, Djakarta or Los Angeles where life has become unbearable, because it takes hours to go from one place to another; cities like Bogota, Johannesburg or Washington DC where crime is rampant; polluted cities like Bucharest or Athens; cities with shanty towns like Rio de Janeiro or Kinshasa; cities of extreme poverty like Calcutta or Bombay.

Given these trends in urban areas, a new urban governance has become essential to ensure social and economic urban development. Before considering what new urban governance and social sustainability might involve, a definition of sustainable urban development and an overview of the evolution of the concept is given in the following sections.

FROM SUSTAINABLE DEVELOPMENT TO SUSTAINABLE URBAN DEVELOPMENT

The concept of sustainable development was attributed its "motto status" in 1987, when the report for the United Nation *Our Common Future*, also known as the Brundtland Report, was published. Making development sustainable was defined as: *"...to ensure that [development] meets the needs of the present without compromising the ability of future generations to meet their own needs."* (World Commission on Environment and Development, 1987, p.8) The concept is not limited to natural and economic resources management, but also has a central social outlook. In particular, sustainable development is a way to deal with widespread poverty: *"...technology and social organisation can be both managed and improved to make way for a new era of economic growth. [...] Sustainable development requires meeting the basic needs of all and extending to all the opportunity to fulfil their aspirations for a better life."* (World Commission on Environment and Development, 1987, p. 8)

In 1993, the European Union included the following definition in its action programme on the environment *(Towards*

Sustainability): "...the word sustainable is used to define a policy and a strategy that encourages continuous social and economic development, without damaging the environment and natural resources, the basis of human activity and future development..." (Commission of the European Communities, 1993)

In this definition, the natural environment concept is extended to the environment in general, and includes human settlements. In its report *Environmental Policies for Cities in the 1990s*, the OECD (1991) indeed stated: *"The challenge posed by this concept of necessity requires cities individually and collectively to contribute to sustainable global development. Cities must therefore always frame their short-term policies in this long-term perspective of evaluating whether and how initiatives contribute to the future development of the global environment..."*

Sustainable urban development became one of the main themes of *Agenda 21*, adopted at the *Earth Summit* in 1992 in Rio de Janeiro. Concern for the future of cities, just as for any other human environment, should include sustainability considerations. These objectives are also developed in several recent papers which give food for thought on improving cultural strategies (Sachs, 1993; Polèse and Stren, 1995) (see Chapter 1.2). They stress the importance of ethical questions, based on the concept of socially sustainable development, integrating notions like social equity, environmental sustainability, economic efficiency and social integration within a context of multiculturalism. A vast and therefore difficult programme to implement.

AN AGENDA FOR SOCIALLY
SUSTAINABLE URBAN POLICIES

How could urban sustainability be tackled operationally? Initially, simple questions can be asked:
- What are the elements that make some cities more liveable than others?
- Why do some cities remain more liveable over a longer period than others?

Both these questions remind us of the important urban context of development: social values, human culture and the environment. Without a contextual vision, no answer is possible. Nonetheless, those questions also lead to a careful analysis: at what level should we analyse these values, cultural and environmental components? At the level of the neighbourhood, city, metropolitan area, or urban region? Each level does indeed generate its own principles: what is intolerable at the neighbourhood level (a main road, for example) may be an absolute necessity for the metropolitan area. An illustration of these contradictory perspectives is the *NIMBY (Not In My Back Yard) Syndrome*, which rejects all potential nuisances, without consideration for the general interest. Should we then only favour the global level, which encompasses the general interest? The contradictions between the international and local perspectives also illustrate the difficulties linked to the global approach.

How should we address these problems? With bottom-up policies, defined by local groups, instead of top-down planning processes? With new regulations to deal with planning disputes based on a co-operative culture? Comparison is useful as many cities are facing a series of challenges for the future which include:
- globalisation and economic restructuring;
- social integration and the refusal to allow fragmentation;
- balanced urban development, within the city and with its hinterland;
- social equity;
- environmental quality;
- new metropolitan governance.

These different challenges can generate contradictory answers. In its policies for sustainable urban management the European Union identifies eight themes for consideration: a competitive and balanced urban system; a dynamic employment market; innovation and know-how; equality and integration; a high quality urban environment; efficient urban transportation; balanced relations between inner cities, suburban and rural areas; and efficient local and urban governance. What would be the most appropriate measures for each of these themes? What would be the most appropriate legislation, the best financial arrangement, and the potential for development?

These questions highlight the need to compare urban management experiences at the outset of the UNESCO/MOST Project on Socially Sustainable Cities.

1.2 Defining Social Sustainability for a City

"Social sustainability for a city is defined as development (and/or growth) that is compatible with the harmonious evolution of civil society, fostering an environment conducive to the compatible cohabitation of culturally and socially diverse groups while at the same time encouraging social integration, with improvements in the quality of life for all segments of the population." (Polèse and Stren, 2000)

This vision of social sustainability *"allows to incorporate others issues related to urban development but that do not always have a direct physical expression and are frequently taken into account in an isolated way: social exclusion, socio-spatial segregation, social citizenship building, urban communities and urban identities, etc. All these issues, like urban poverty, are at the core of urban governance relations and must be incorporated by the new urban planning approach as well as traditional issues like housing, transportation, urban services, public spaces and economic development."* (Lungo, Cape Town Conference Papers 1998)

"In principle, sustainability is not limited to ecological and economic sustenance; it also encompasses health and other social dimensions. These dimensions are considered together with the capacity of the built environment to adapt to predictable and unforeseen events and gradual changes within and from outside cities. The term social sustainability will be interpreted as the capacity of a human group, institution or society to deal with environmental, economic, health or other kinds of problems in order to promote the quality of life for current and future generations." (Lawrence, Cape Town Conference Papers 1998)

CONSIDERING KEY LOCAL MANAGEMENT THEMES

To allow consideration of local policies beyond any contextual differences, the MOST Network has chosen six main themes for discussion:
- urban governance;
- social and cultural policies;
- public services;
- land and housing policies;
- urban transport;
- economic revitalisation.

Without claiming to cover all urban management policies, the analysis of these key issues allows us to consider solutions that could promote socially sustainable cities.

Each theme is introduced in the following chapters with a discussion of conceptual elements and general urban management issues. Examples drawn from the Network's case studies then illustrate how these issues have been tackled in local and metropolitan policies.

CHAPTER 2

Urban governance

The Concept of Urban Governance

"Governance is understood here as the relationship between State and civil society (McCarney, Halfani and Rodríguez, 1995). Theoretically then, civil society's participation is indispensable to build democratic urban governance relations." (Lungo, Cape Town Conference Papers 1998)

GOVERNANCE TAILORED FOR METROPOLITAN PROBLEMS

Many cities are divided according to multiple institutional and spatial structures inherited from the past, and have diverging competence and interests. Efficient urban management and local governance are at the centre of various debates focusing on finding coherent and global urban policies which respect the diversity of urban communities. Are there insoluble conflicts between the various urban divides — city centre/suburbs; concentration/decentralisation; spatial equity/economic disparities? Do centralised metropolitan management mechanisms provide a better governance environment than other devolved and democratic systems?

The emergence of social movements and community interest groups is a signal of dissatisfaction with present urban management practices, questioning the efficiency of local authorities and their potential to resolve general or local problems, such as that of exclusion, unemployment and urban rehabilitation.

Ways to manage cities evolve rapidly because of contradictions within the urban system. Should wealthy suburbs only finance their own services, with no concern for centres that are degrading owing to a lack of employment and resources? The North American urban model has failed, even in Toronto where a municipal reorganisation has occurred at a level that is too limited. Emerging "edge cities" — the new suburban towns — reflect the desertion of the central city by a portion of the economic and social forces. The European model has also generated problems, with large social housing estates adjacent to wealthy suburbs. In addition, most Third World cities, fragmented into districts of rapid immigration around a degrading city-centre, have not yet found sustainable management structures. In Nairobi, for example, a governance crisis has become evident, but ways to overcome it are still to be found. Budapest, San Salvador, Lyon and Cape Town have taken strong measures: Cape Metropolitan Council has grouped former municipalities under one urban authority; in Budapest, reorganisation in suburban municipalities permits a new form of metropolitan governance; in San Salvador and Lyon participatory planning initiatives have been developed.

A new global governance of cities is essential for a better distribution of wealth and problems. Such governance implies devising cross-cutting approaches between different policies, thinking at different geographical levels and formally defining policy implementation strategies among the partners involved. It is therefore essential to propose policies in terms of stakeholders, scale and context in order to promote equity, efficiency and sustainability. Planning priorities can thus be devised "associating political institutions, social stakeholders and private organisations in policy definition and implementation processes based on collective choices that generate an active adhesion of citizens". (Ascher, 1995, p. 269)

FROM GOVERNANCE CRISIS
TO PARTNERSHIP BUILDING

Nairobi has experienced three successive social transformations with different implications in terms of social and spatial exclusion. These impacts are examined by Diana Lee-Smith and Davinder Lamba both historically and sectorally in relation to land and transport (see also Chapters 4 and 6). Their analysis shows that *"none of these social transformations have so far been conducive to social sustainability."*

At present, Nairobi is undergoing a governance crisis (see Chapter 2.1) which is manifest in conflicts over resources and power sharing among a variety of urban stakeholders. This crisis calls for *"some form of accommodation between these competing interests and co-operation between governmental and non-governmental actors."* For this to emerge *"demands a considerable balancing act of the powerful forces at work."* The main question raised is whether these forces are likely to *"lead to greater social sustainability through better governance, or whether Nairobi will become a victim of forces of social disintegration."*

Budapest has faced several urban governance problems during its recent history. György Enyedi examines *"how legislation and the system of urban governance responded to key issues that were created by urban growth and suburbanisation; and how social tensions and their management have been changed during the post-socialist transition since 1990."*

The different stages through which governance in Budapest has evolved provide *"an example of how urban governance could follow the sudden transition from an authoritarian political system to a democratic one."* The approach that is presented *"is not political but rather practical: how urban governance should change its institutions, goal-setting process, planning procedures etc. during such a transition."*

The main issue considered in the Budapest case study (see Chapter 2.2) is the sharing of power between the city of Budapest and its suburban area: *"the lack of co-ordinated government between the city of Budapest and its suburban zone has been a continuous problem for planning the development of the Metropolitan Area since the end of the last century."*

In **San Salvador**, the complexity of urban governance has had major impacts on metropolitan planning. Mario Lungo stresses that: *"the complexity of metropolitan area development creates a multiplicity of tasks that render a multiplicity of institutions inevitable. Additionally most of the metropolitan cities have a multi-municipal composition. Establishing a metropolitan perspective is thus an arduous process."* The challenge, therefore, is *"to find the urban development issues (environment, poverty,*

violence or globalisation process), which combine both munici-
pal and metropolitan interests; and to establish participatory
mechanisms for actors who work at different levels (neighbour-
hood, city, metropolitan, national, international)."

The case of San Salvador Metropolitan Area (see Chapter 2.3)
illustrates how different attempts have been made to develop participatory planning and consensus building processes. *"The main*
problems identified in terms of urban governance are both the
lack of metropolitan management institutions and the absence
of a social metropolitan identity among most of the urban
actors." Mario Lungo stresses, however, that *"some metropolitan*
problems are a useful way to stimulate and to promote the con-
struction of social identities. For example the introduction of
environmental dimensions in metropolitan planning was used in
San Salvador as a mechanism to build urban governance rela-
tions by establishing consensus among different actors around
this problem."

In **Lyon**, urban policies have focused on urban renewal designed
for suburban disadvantaged neighbourhoods. Bruno Voisin notes
that Lyon has implemented genuine development policy, *"bringing*
a balanced conurbation-wide approach but also concerning the
day-to-day lives of those living in the most disadvantaged areas."
"Maintaining social links therefore goes hand in hand with
respecting the environmental balance, pursuing economic devel-
opment and controlling urban sprawl as one of the most impor-
tant of the conurbation's policy areas." (see also Chapter 7)

How can violence in suburban neighbourhoods be dealt with?
Which urban policy can be undertaken to reskill socially deprived
areas? Lyon's experience (see Chapter 2.5) illustrate the potential
of participatory programmes and of self-governance in getting people to be responsible for running their local area. *"The need to*
rejuvenate the large local authority housing areas and let their
inhabitants play a full role in the economic and cultural devel-
opment of the urban area is the same as the need to ensure sus-
tainable development by halting the factors that have caused
imbalance and fragmentation within the metropolitan area."

Another aim of self-governance is *"to reforge the social links*
in an area blighted by poverty and social exclusion by involving
the residents who are most disadvantaged and who have suf-
fered most with unemployment in looking after their urban
environment." But *"how should we act on a voluntary basis in*

an ambitious and long-term manner to involve all the public and private partners concerned in fighting social and urban imbalances and the dramatic effects these imbalances have on the most disadvantaged populations?" Moreover, *"how can we ensure that residents are not just the passive recipients of measures to improve their conditions and lifestyle, but that the citizens involved in these cases become the driving force of this social change and active partners in public action?"* Bruno Voisin suggests setting up *"genuine partnerships involving several different groups, and giving significant space to the residents of the neighbourhoods concerned."*

Three examples of local participation are presented *"which, first of all, have the merit of having lasted a long time and having produced social changes in the neighbourhoods where they took place."*

In **Cape Town**, the implementation of new urban institutional structures has been a central element of urban governance for the Cape Metropolitan Area. Stewart Fisher presents the new sharing of powers and duties: *"Prior to the democratisation of South Africa in 1994, there were 39 political local government bodies in the Cape Metropolitan Area. The area is now governed by the Cape Metropolitan Council (CMC), and six Metropolitan Local Councils."*

The current situation these metropolitan authorities have to face is challenging: poverty and inequality, a large and growing population, major gaps in basic services provision, unemployment and a major housing shortage.

An *Integrated Development Plan (IDP)* has been established as *"the process and tool that is driving the formulation of policy in the Cape Metropole."* (see Chapter 2.4) *"The IDP framework should be used as a guideline for the business planning and budgeting processes in both the CMC and Metropolitan Local Councils. Furthermore it can provide the basis on which local government can report to the metropolitan community regarding its priorities, its intentions and the basis on which its performance can be assessed. It can also be the starting point for more detailed long-term strategy work and implementation planning."*

The author concludes that *"good governance is being recognised as a crucial element of successful project implementation and the achievement of social harmony at a local level, whereas at the policy level the emphasis has been on partnership between the CMC and the six Municipalities. In fact, both of these are components of good governance, which need to be integrated at a policy level."*

On a more conceptual level, **Geneviève Dubois-Taine** discusses why urban policies since World War II have often failed to manage urban territories (see Chapter 2.6). She stresses that society has undergone major changes and that *"new urban values emerge in the peripheries of the towns."* Thus *"if urban areas are to be managed in a realistic way, it is a necessity to know and share these new values."*

On the basis of a research study intiled *"New Values for Future Urban Planning"*, the author proposes three examples that *"explain how new forces and values impact on our urban territories and illustrate the importance of developing a new urban culture."*

2.1 Nairobi's Social Transformations and Governance Crisis

from Diana Lee-Smith and Davinder Lamba, *"Social Transformation in a Post-Colonial City: The Case of Nairobi"*

Successive Social Transformations: From Ethnic to Economic Exclusion

The first transformation in Nairobi began in 1896 with the founding of the colonial city and the imposition of norms which set out to exclude the local population.

Africans were legally prevented from owning freehold property in the city until the 1920s. Thereafter the settlers prevented such ownership through zoning and social pressures (see Figure 2.1). Segregation was extended to education and cultural amenities. Extensive land alienation led to the Mau Mau, or Kenya Land Freedom Army, guerrilla struggle of the 1950s.

The second transformation occurred with independence in 1963 and the creation of a multi-ethnic African state. The policy of social exclusion also continued, but based on income rather than ethnicity, with a class division between those living in suburban estates and the dispossessed class.

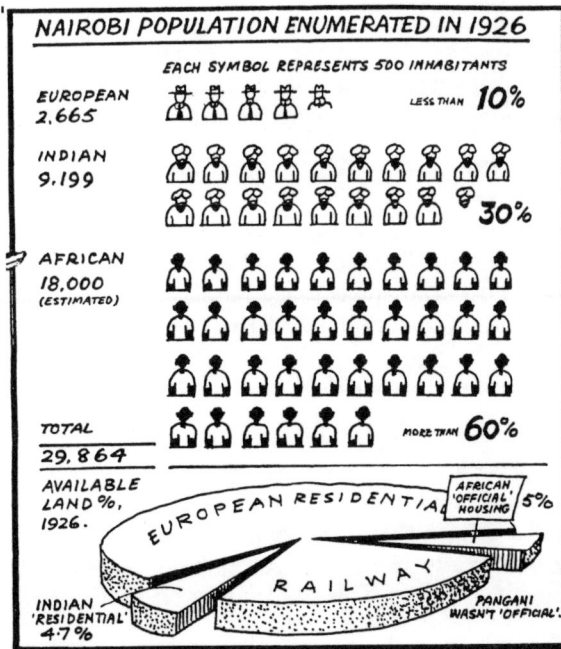

NAIROBI POPULATION ENUMERATED IN 1926

EACH SYMBOL REPRESENTS 500 INHABITANTS

EUROPEAN 2,665 — LESS THAN 10%

INDIAN 9,199 — 30%

AFRICAN 18,000 (ESTIMATED) — MORE THAN 60%

TOTAL 29,864

AVAILABLE LAND %, 1926.

EUROPEAN RESIDENTIAL

AFRICAN 'OFFICIAL' HOUSING 5%

RAILWAY

INDIAN 'RESIDENTIAL' 4.7%

PANGANI WASN'T 'OFFICIAL'.

Source: Hirst and Lamba (1994)

Figure 2.1 **Unequal Share of Available Land in Colonial Nairobi:** *city population and land distribution in 1926*

In terms of local governance, the Nairobi City Council became a forum for local representatives elected by residents of the various neighbourhoods. While the council was granted extensive new responsibilities, new city councillors had no previous experience of local government. Municipal finance emerged as a major problem.

The removal of colonial restrictions on freedom of movement at independence meant a rapid increase in rural-urban migration. Efforts made to address the needs of the growing population were largely ineffective, and the "self-help city" grew like a balloon.

As a result, Nairobi still reflects its segregationist heritage with regard to planning, amenities and administration. The middle-class residential areas now house a racial mix and have both extended and densified. The old "native" housing areas are still there, and the city has extended further to the east with new housing and unauthorised settlements. The populations here are predominantly African and low income.

Tensions between central and local government reflect the struggle for control over the resources of the wealthiest area of the country. Central government has maintained control of the city's administration and has removed various revenue generating sources from the City Council. Central government also has to approve any measure increasing those still under local jurisdiction. Until 1983, when the City Council was dissolved due to "gross mismanagement and poor delivery of services," the city was largely dependent on the government for grants to supplement its own meagre resources

The third transformation is considered to have begun with national multi-party elections in 1992. This transformation is characterised by civil society activism for social reform on a broad front, including civic reform. Through a combination of coercion and manipulation, central government virtually paralysed the operations of the city government in the period 1993-1997.

A Governance Crisis and Pressure for Change

A system of governance that involves all the key players in government and civil society is essential to resolve the current conflicts and contradictions in Nairobi. The latter are rooted in a system that militates against social sustainability by excluding what is now the majority of the population of the city from civic recognition and by pitting diverse groups against each other. This has led to a crisis of governance.

Nairobi's institutions are currently locked in a battle for power that is eroding the capacity of its citizens to manage the wealth concentrated in the city. Nairobi's s history of exclusion has structured the way institutions operate as much, or more, than it has structured physical space.

The city councillors' powers are in fact limited by the control central government has over the appointments of heads of departments. Perhaps even more important, the map of Nairobi is overlaid with the alternative institutional framework of the provincial administration. This administrative structure, inherited from colonial times, was challenged in 1997 by the civil society reform movement. Conflicts between the provincial administration and various interest groups in the City have escalated during 1998.

The ability of residents in the informal slum areas to address their needs has been greatly restricted. Until late 1991, the KANU (Kenya African National Union) offices in each area worked with committees of community elders and the district administration. With the advent of multi-partyism, those links were weakened; the administrative structure, however, remained in place. In 1997, efforts to develop local governance structures in one informal slum area were broken up by the chief with police reinforcement. Despite the removal of a legal prohibition on meetings of ten or more persons without permission of the local chief, the provincial administration continues to break up meetings of its choice on the pretext that "notification" which is now required has not been correctly given.

Sectoral groups have also been subjected to similar controls. However, during the pressure for social reforms in the mid-1990s, numerous groups have reasserted themselves and the prospects for organising formal- and informal-sector interest groups to represent their members' interests are improving as the pressure for reforms continues.

Kenya's system of government has not always acted as an agent of law and order. On the contrary, the provincial and district administration personnel have been instrumental in structuring Nairobi's informal settlements, and in administering these areas of social exclusion outside the legal framework of the formal city (see Chapter 4.1 for details). The divide between city and central government officialdom is certainly not clear cut in this respect, with many, if not most, city officials colluding in these activities, which also conveniently provide them with income in the form of bribes.

The socially excluded groups in Nairobi rely for most of their services on assistance from NGOs. Religious organisations also play an important role in supporting these communities. The number and range of such support activities has increased rapidly in recent years, although data is limited.

Pressures for urban reform were already expressed in the preparations for the 1992 multi-party elections, when several political parties combined to articulate a post-election platform that incorporated several sectors affecting Nairobi, including housing and other aspects of social exclusion. However, the common platform was submerged in the scramble for power. Such reforms were subsequently articulated in the Nairobi City Convention, which included inputs from a wide spectrum of urban interests. Again, the programme, which included a halt to demolitions, the extension of services to informal settlements and a reform of building codes, was submerged in political infighting.

The potential participants in a system of governance that would make for a more socially sustainable city are not engaged in any form of either negotiation or setting of goals that might contribute towards such a system. All that exists in the late 1990s is some movement towards the formation of more community-based and sectoral civic organisations that might have the potential at some stage in the future to define their different interests and achieve their strategic goals.

Co-operation or Conflict?

In order for Nairobi's excluded majority to participate in the city's governance, the current social transformation must work its way through towards greater democracy. This is already ongoing in the form of pressure for social reform, although the nature of a new system of governance and how it will be established is not clear. Such a system needs to be based in the dispossessed neighbourhoods and to reinvigorate Nairobi City Council from below.

There are calls for neighbourhood associations which have formal recognition and a defined relationship to local government to articulate their demands. How are these demands going to be achieved in relation to the existing structures of laws and administration?

There are also calls for residents with grievances to organise local chapters and to campaign within the confines of the law. However, violations of the law backed by the authorities are so blatant that numerous communities have resorted to pulling down illegal structures and fences.

There is, finally, an opportunity for the high- and middle-income neighbourhoods to chart the course for a more inclusive system of governance, which could possibly provide a model for the excluded neighbourhoods. Should this occur, social forces within the city could have opened up the required political space for a new balance of power and greater social inclusiveness. A more democratic system of local governance would have the potential for social sustainability through inclusion and distribution of benefits to various groups. However, it will first be necessary for central government to move from its present position of intransigence to accommodate more interests in the city.

2.2 Decentralisation *vs.* Metropolitan Management in Budapest

from György Enyedi, *"Budapest Metropolitan Region"*

Four Periods of Economic and Political Changes

Budapest's metropolitan development has followed changes in the economic and political systems that have taken place in the country. These are: the birth of a modern capital city and its metropolitan area (1873-1914); the ideas about Greater Budapest and the first decrees for metropolitan planning (1920-1945); the socialist era (1945-1990); the post-socialist transition (after 1990)

These 130 years of metropolitan development show that:
- Budapest has always had a special importance within the country as an economic centre, as the authoritative centre and as the only metropolis.
- Whereas the capital city has been carefully planned and modernised, the suburban zone has remained neglected.
- Despite several attempts, the planning and development of the whole metropolitan area have never succeeded, because of the resistance of either Budapest or the suburban settlements, or both.
- The relation between the capital city and its suburban zone has been characterised by the dominance of Budapest, instead of by consensus and co-operation. This has developed a strong suspicion in the suburban settlements, which has sometimes led to resistance to any sort of co-operation.

The Present Dilemmas of Metropolitan Governance

In the post-socialist transition since 1990, the most important changes in Budapest have been the following:
- *a reform of the local government system*, including a special law on the capital city of Budapest;
- *a functional restructuring of the city*: the return of international functions; industrial relocation; concentration of high level business services;
- *a transformation of the suburban zone*: the development of upper middle class suburbs; the partial relocation from the city of industrial, commercial and other space consuming activities.
- since Budapest Metropolitan Development Council was established in 1996, the metropolitan area has an official statistical definition (Budapest plus 78 municipalities).

The Local Government System

In 1990, a new Act on Local Governments was passed by the new, democratically elected parliament. This regulation gave the same legal status to each municipality, abolished all sorts of hierarchical order in public administration and made the municipalities responsible for almost all local government tasks.

There was a separate act concerning Budapest's local government, which remained a two-tier one. The 23 districts became the primary decision-making level. They were obliged to provide most of the public services. They were attributed the right to make local decrees, to provide construction permits, and they also became the owners of the municipal land and housing stock. The law granted only a limited right of regulation to the capital city. Even the financing of common tasks (e.g. urban transport) became a subject of negotiation. Following the principle of subsidiarity, the capital city mostly received those functions which the districts were unable to carry out.

The strong position of the districts had advantageous effects in the legitimisation of local governments, in inviting civil organisations to participate in decision-making and in mobilising local initiatives and local resources. At the same time, the integrating power of the capital city had weakened, the legal framework for integrated urban service provision and urban planning was lacking. The negative consequences of administrative disintegration became evident: debates between the districts and the capital city; resistance of suburban municipalities to any influence of Budapest; the impossibility of working out a housing policy or a new Master Plan for Budapest, let alone the metropolitan area.

The Act on Local Governments was modified in 1994. The capital city remained a two-tier government, but the modification created hierarchical conditions within the city. The competence attributed to the capital city reflects the priorities given to the economies of scale, efficiency, and to the needs of integrated urban management. Budapest is authorised to work out the urban development, urban renewal and physical plans, and is responsible for housing management control, environmental protection, public transport and the provision of car parking facilities in the districts.

The Impact of Regional Policy on Metropolitan Integration

The Act on Regional Development and Physical Planning (1996) created an institutional system that was aimed at integrating development in the agglomeration around Budapest (see Figure 2.2). *Development Councils* were set up as partnership institutions in all

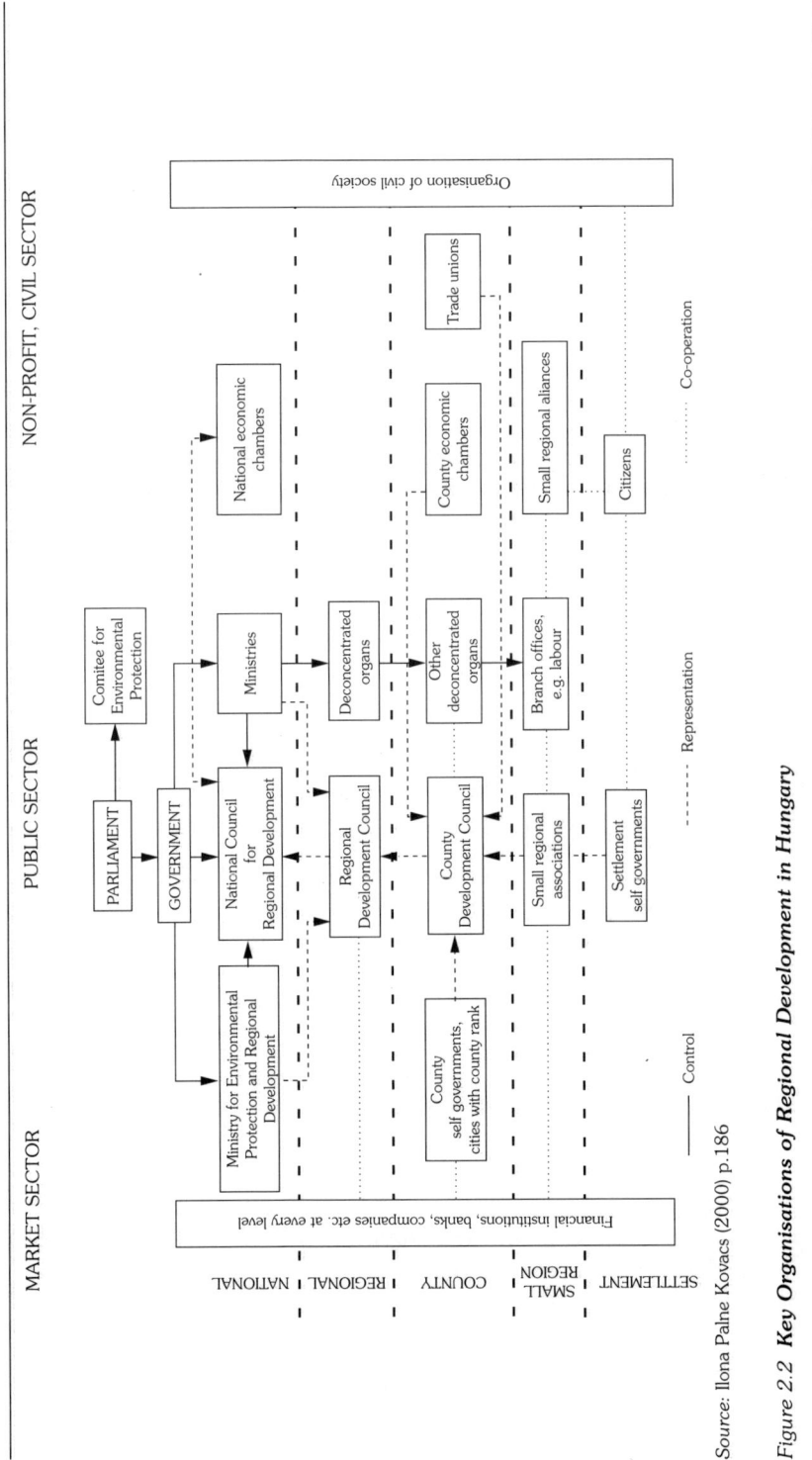

Source: Ilona Palne Kovacs (2000) p.186

Figure 2.2 **Key Organisations of Regional Development in Hungary**

counties. They consist of the representatives of local governments; chambers of commerce; industry and agriculture; organisations of employees and the government. These bodies decide upon the development programmes of the counties and the distribution of the state development subsidies. The Act enabled the formation of *Regional Development Councils* based on the voluntary associations of county Development Councils, and stipulated the compulsory creation of such a Council in the Budapest agglomeration.

Metropolitan Budapest has now 24 local authorities within the city and 78 in the suburban zone. From the point of view of regional development, a suburban commune is under the competence of the Pest County Development Council and also under that of the Budapest Metropolitan Development Council. It may also belong to one (or more) micro-regional development associations, even to the (not yet established) Budapest Region, designated as a *NUTS 2 Region* of the European Union (a subdivision of the Nomenclature of Territorial Units for Statistics).

The *Budapest Metropolitan Development Council*, with its chairman delegated by central government, and with representatives of nine ministries as members, shows the domination of the national government and the representation of many conflicting interests. Furthermore, its authority is limited, its derived competence being based on the agreement between Budapest and the Development Council of Pest County. The development concept of Metropolitan Budapest also requires the approval of central government.

The Budapest Metropolitan Development Council is, however, the first organisation which formally integrates the capital city, the districts, the suburban settlements and the county, together with the government and different economic interest groups. This Council may become the centre for organising regional integration in the Budapest metropolitan area, without any unified public administration system.

Operational Features of Budapest Governance

A Macro-political Dimension

Budapest has a closer relation to the government than any other municipality. What happens in Budapest is often of national significance. Consequently, central government takes part in infrastructure investments and the capital city can apply for specific government subsidies for urban development. However, these investments are directly controlled by the government and the development of the capital city has been influenced by the political consent (or conflict) existing between the national government and the city's authorities.

Internal Power Conditions

Owing to many conflicting interests, municipal governments are good training fields for politicians to learn how to reach consensus and compromise. Conflicts have developed between the City and the districts, but districts are divided among themselves too. The peripheral districts, where large social housing estates are located, oppose the development of the rich central districts.

Voluntary Co-operation in Social Policy

Social policy is the first field where solidarity and co-operation have become stronger than rivalry. The Social Charter of Budapest was signed by the mayors of the city and 23 districts in 1997. It integrates social policy stakeholders at different levels and from different sectors, and deals with poverty, social exclusion, marginalisation and weak social integration. This new approach is based on dialoguing with civil organisations, strengthening family and community ties, and promoting individual capacities.

Citizen-friendly Governance — Basic Democracy

The Act on Local Governments gives to the inhabitants a *sui generis* right to participate in local decision-making and regulates several direct forms of democracy (e.g. referenda and community initiatives).

Budapest's civil society is well organised: one third of the 50,000 civil organisations in Hungary operate in Budapest. They are especially active in the fields of social policy, environmental protection, conservation of the built environment, and culture. These organisations combine Budapest and the suburban zone in their activities only in exceptional cases.

Minority local governments represent an interesting transition between civil organisations and local governments. They articulate the interests of ethnic minorities and can participate in local government decision-making; hence their positions are stronger than those of civil associations. In 1994, during the ethnic minority governmental elections, 7 minority governments were established at the capital city level and another 43 at the district level.

2.3 Developing Democratic Urban Governance in San Salvador Metropolitan Area

from Mario Lungo, *"Metropolitan Planning and Civil Society Participation: Developing Urban Governance in El Salvador"*

The Context of Urban Governance

In El Salvador, the role of civil society organisations in urban development has been broad since the economic adjustment programmes and the disengagement from social policy implementation by the central government. It has allowed the transfer of services to local authorities; the participation of non-governmental and private sectors in social programmes; and greater levels of participation of community-based associations in local decision-making processes.

However, urban governance in San Salvador Metropolitan Area (SSMA) has been difficult because of the following factors:
- *a limited degree of decentralisation*: resistance on the part of central government to delegating decision-making power to municipalities and to giving full financial autonomy to local authorities;
- *technocratic urban planning continues to be dominant*: plans are the result of the work of small groups of technicians with only informational-level public participation;
- *clientelism* remains the main way for political parties to relate to the population;
- *a lack of a metropolitan social identity*.

These negative factors could be reversed with effective metropolitan governance, for instance with the development of metropolitan structures and of public participation.

The San Salvador Metropolitan Council of Mayors, which has acted since 1994, has its own San Salvador Metropolitan Planning Office (OPAMSS). This kind of partial metropolitan government has been very useful to address problems that surpass local municipal capacities, like waste management. It has additional potential to manage urban problems like water provision, public transportation and citizen security at the metropolitan scale.

The development of public participation in metropolitan planning would also constitute a useful instrument for the construction of new urban governance relations with a democratic and participatory character.

METROPLAN 80: A Gap in Local Participation

The first SSMA Master Plan, known as METROPLAN 80, was a technocratic product. It was guided by the dominant urban concept: building a "dreamed city" with appropriate patterns of urban space organisation and almost imperceptible social divides. The centralising and repressive State further reinforced the technocratic vision in its attempt to implement the plan.

Citizen participation was limited to two spheres: the elaboration of the plan, through political process or via community representatives who acted as advisors; and, exceptionally, the execution of specific projects.

METROPLAN 80 proposed a confusing concept of social partici- pation, which was both restrictive and exclusive. It did not differentiate between governmental and non-governmental actors; it did not pro- pose citizens' participatory mechanisms and was therefore ignored by the majority of the population.

PLAMADUR 1997: A Timid Civil Participation

The SSMA Development Plan, known as PLAMADUR, was pro- duced in a different socio-political context and appeared more realistic and democratic. PLAMADUR considered participation important in the decision-making process, looked for efficient forms of consensus and participation of the business sector, citizens, and civil servants. Some of its principles are the following:

- *use of another model of urban development:* instead of a monocentric metropolitan area, a polycentric model is proposed to diminish primacy of San Salvador within SSMA;
- *usefulness of the plan* for the whole society, in terms of eco- nomic development and the quality of life;
- *formulation of strategic objectives*, precise and easy to under- stand;
- *demonstration of the feasibility* of the goals within the pre- dicted time-frames;
- *participation and shared responsibility of citizens*, with clear and equal rules for all, transparency in decision-making;
- *broad and permanent communication.*

However, the limited citizen participation in PLAMADUR's elabo- ration phase indicates that the plan was insufficiently disseminated. The proposal also lacked mechanisms to build consensus. Those put in place to get feedback did not work (events, workshops, "consensus forums").

A number of facts have also limited municipal government participation in PLAMADUR:

- the plan emerged from central government without participation
  from local governments. Moreover, the Mayor of San Salvador
  failed to demonstrate ownership of the project;
- the question of urban development still does not have an important position in the national agenda and the plan lacked a wide
  dissemination programme;
- the Plan's design gave privilege to the discussion with technical
  experts of central government, lacked power to make strategic
  decisions, and excluded civil society organisations.

PLAMADUR has therefore been an incomplete effort to break
away from the conception of technocratic urban planning.

Widening Municipal and Social Participation in PLAMADUR

The discussion process of PLAMADUR began in early 1998,
mainly for two reasons: (i) the triumph of the left-wing political parties
in the majority of San Salvador Metropolitan Municipalities and (ii) the
public debate provoked by the decision of the SSMA Council to sus-
pend the construction of various urbanisation projects based on their
negative environmental impact. The discussion focused on the use of
urban and suburban land in the metropolitan area, and allowed diver-
gent positions to be expressed by various city actors, who until now
had not sat down at the same table.

Nevertheless, there are many issues still to be to resolved, including:

- *promoting social participation* of NGOs, urban community-
  based and business associations, in policy formulation for urban
  planning, and not only in project execution;
- *strengthening the capacity* of municipal authorities in city and
  metropolitan planning, especially regarding current privatisation
  and decentralisation processes;
- *building metropolitan social identities*; without them, any
  effort to consolidate the incipient metropolitan institutions like
  the SSMA Council will fail.

PLAMADUR has initiated a consensus process between the State
and civil society about the city's future, which now has to be built upon.

2.4   Integrated Planning in the Cape Metropolitan Area

from Stewart Fisher, *"Integrated Development Planning in the Cape Metropolitan Area"*

A Metropolitan Integrated Development Planning Process

Since 1996, each South African metropolitan council is required to formulate and implement a metropolitan Integrated Development Plan (IDP) which incorporates land-use planning, transport planning, infrastructure planning and integrated economic development. In 1997 the Cape Metropolitan Council (CMC) together with the six Metropolitan Local Councils (see Figure 2.3) initiated such an integrated development planning process. A Metropolitan Co-ordinating Forum has been established with political representatives from all the Councils and civil society, and with technical advisors to co-ordinate and monitor local development plans.

The IDP planning process involves an annual cycle of planning, action and review to enable Councils to align or integrate their activities and resources in a strategic, accountable and cost efficient manner. This is to be achieved through a *four-phase process*:

- *Phase 1 Setting Direction:* agreeing on a vision for the Cape Metropolitan Area; analysing the metropolitan reality and identifying key strategic themes.
- *Phase 2 Formulating Strategy:* addressing each strategic priority; developing financial and organisation strategies; integrating and aligning the strategic priority.
- *Phase 3 Developing Implementation Plans:* setting objectives; defining priority programmes and projects with agreed targets; preparing 3-5-year action plans and detailed 1-year action plans with key performance indicators; costing the programmes and projects; implementing the plans and reviewing them on an ongoing basis.
- *Phase 4 Monitoring, Reviewing and Revising:* a process of assessing performance against the agreed targets, and revising where targets are not met.

Five Key IDP Themes

- *Targeting poverty and homelessness*: to reduce the percentage of the population living in poverty through mobilising the resources of local government, of the community and of other agencies. Central in this regard is to extend the provision of education and skills training to the poor.

- *Strengthening the Cape Metropole's global economic position:* to create an attractive investment climate through the development of entrepreneurial skills, the promotion of tourism, regenerating and supporting a strong integrating cultural life, and improving safety and security.

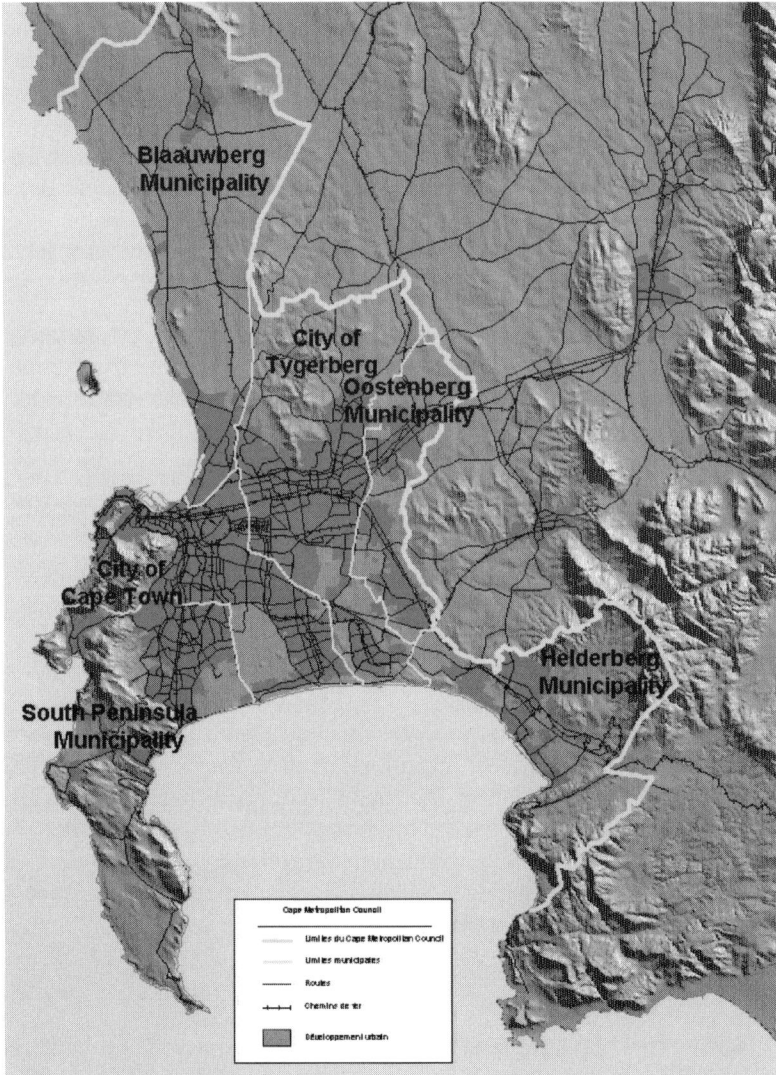

Source: Cape Metropolitan Council

Figure 2.3 **Cape Metropolitan Local Authorities:** *a longitudinal administrative division to avoid concentrating suburban problems in peripheral municipalities*

- *Enhancing the environment*: to create a safe, pleasant, healthy living and natural environment, by providing basic services to all and by developing "green" areas, recycling and sustainable utilisation practices.
- *Building social harmony and civic responsibility*: to build a more harmonious society and a greater civic responsibility, tackling crime and increasing safety and security, promoting civic education and public involvement in local government and community issues.
- *Developing local government*: to build an efficient, effective, innovative and sustainable system of local government which responds to the needs of the community in a democratic and cooperative manner.

Five Key CMC Projects

The Metropolitan Spatial Development Framework

In 1991 a programme of establishing a system of overarching spatial plans was initiated by Cape metropolitan authorities. The plan so drafted was termed the *Metropolitan Spatial Development Framework* (MSDF). The MSDF aims to redress the unequal distribution of, and access to, employment by directing public and private investment into areas of greatest need. Key intervention areas are corridors and nodes where mixed land-use is encouraged, as well as strategies to enhance the environment. The MSDF aims to provide clarity in respect to the form and location of future spatial growth, integrate socially and economically the disparate communities of the metropolitan area and develop local participatory processes (see Chapter 5.1 for details on this project).

Moving Ahead: Cape Metropolitan Transport Plan

To fully integrate the various elements of transport, the *Moving Ahead* process was initiated in 1995. Based on the MSDF spatial plan, the metropolitan integrated transport plan targets the key IDP themes: by providing affordable public transport and promoting social housing along transport corridors; by developing the transport network and encouraging the use of public transport (see Chapter 6.2 for details on this project).

Economic Development Framework

An *Economic Development Framework (EDF)* was initiated by the CMC to develop and implement a holistic framework for addressing economic growth and poverty alleviation, and to promote sustainable urban development. The EDF aims to achieve agreed integrated economic and social development objectives, to co-ordinate the strategic economic development activities of the CMC and of metropolitan local authorities, and to outline a decision-making framework for the allocation of resources (see Chapter 8.1 for details on this project).

Housing Needs Analysis

A *Housing Department* was established late in 1997 to co-ordinate housing development strategies at the metropolitan level. Based on the MSDF, the strategy is mainly achieved through the establishment of inter-municipal and role-player forums.

Environmental Policy

The *Environmental Management Department* was established late in 1997 to draft an all-embracing environmental strategy. A State of the Environment Report should be published in 1999 and will be followed by a draft environmental policy. Bio-physical issues dominate the environmental debate in the Cape Metropole. This is understandable to some extent, given that the metropolitan area contains the only national park in the world to be surrounded by a city. Hence the primary focus here is to ensure the continued attraction of tourists needed to underpin the region's economy.

Linkages Between Metropolitan Projects and IDP Themes

Three major benefits are emerging from the key metropolitan projects in terms of their efficacy in addressing the IDP themes. These benefits relate to: *data collection* to quantify the socio-economic situation within the Cape Metropole; *spatial integration* to address the spatial inequalities; and a much clearer understanding of the *global economic reality*.

A number of important linkages should be made, including: monitoring and understanding the inter-relationship between the metropolitan projects; growth management links with the budget; the relationship between policy and implementation itself.

IDP Implications for Metropolitan and Local Authorities

Emerging issues

- The activities of national, provincial and local authorities all have ultimately the same focal point — community life. This points to the need for a comprehensive stakeholder analysis and concerted efforts to ensure representation.

- The budget needs to be directly linked to the IDP process.
- Technical task teams ought to think about the impact of their deliberations on each of the strategic themes; likewise each of the working groups that are in operation. Cross-functional task teams could be part of the solution.
- The IDP cannot be viewed as a technical process free of political influence. It must take into account the development needs and priorities as determined by the local councils, which presupposes a certain level of co-operative government between the local councils and the Cape Metropolitan Council.

Relationship between the CMC and the Municipalities

Within the Cape metropolitan structure, responsibility for the co-ordinating policy lies with the CMC, while the Municipalities are responsible for the implementation. When analysed from a CMC policy perspective, the core focus is constructed around poverty alleviation and economic growth. The areas of social harmony and local government development are dependent upon the successful implementation of the former. On the other hand, when the same set of themes is viewed from the perspective of the Municipalities, with their responsibility for implementation, the key themes then become those of social harmony (with the concerns about crime uppermost) and the issue of governance. From a policy perspective, it is important to adopt a set of strategies for implementation that are based upon medium- to long-term goals, as this ultimately ensures the most effective use of limited resources. When charged with the responsibility for implementation in the face of stark immediate need, however, the greatest priority is to address the areas of immediate need. Hence the emerging distinction around the themes.

The Financial Implications

As economic growth is less than the population growth rate, the income level per capita is falling, placing an increasing strain on the budget. A Financial Framework Task Team, representing the different local authorities of the Cape Metropole, has been established to create a single, rational metropolitan-wide approach to financial management.

Financial capacity is clearly an important area that has to be taken into account in setting policy. In theory the CMC can use its distribution powers to support those areas of activity identified by the IDP process. In practice, however, this can only work if there is surplus funding available. In this regard there are valuable lessons to be drawn from the approach adopted by the *Economic Development Framework* (see Chapter 7.1), which sees the role of local government as a facilitator rather than as an agent of intervention.

2.5   Local Governance in Lyon's Deprived Neighbourhoods

from Bruno Voisin, *"Social Development and Local Governance in Greater Lyon"*

Uneven Urban Development and Social Imbalance

The Lyon conurbation is France's second largest urban area after Paris and its suburbs. Pronounced geographical contrasts, especially between the east and west of Greater Lyon, underlie the social imbalance within the city.

Between 1950 and 1980, rapid economic growth made it necessary to accommodate immigrants from both rural France and developing countries. The working population from various origins was housed in huge residential areas hastily planned and built in East Lyon. The transition from the industrial era to the services-dominated period over the last twenty years has only exacerbated these imbalances. The disadvantaged populations have tended to concentrate in the large areas of local authority housing. This has led to social conflicts and urban violence, accelerating the disadvantages of these areas. The salaried middle classes, workers and skilled employees tend to leave these neighbourhoods and move to the residential areas of the outer periphery.

To redress the balance, the Urban Community — a structure of inter-communal co-operation bringing together 55 communes of the conurbation — has instigated since 1990 a set of conurbation-wide priority policies. The "City Contract," for instance, is the basis of an active partnership between the State, Region, Department and the Urban Community, to re-skill areas of local authority housing (see Chapter 7.2 for details). Policy emphasis has also been placed on local governance and resident participation in local decision-making.

Beyond Formal Consultation and Representation

The weight of problems faced by a segregated population, lacking economic security, stuck in their current living environment, diverse in their ethnic identity, places of origin and cultural points of reference, raises the question "How can residents themselves get to act on behalf of the authorities?" What structures need to be put in place to promote self-governance and integrate a diverse society, to build dialogue, mutual respect and promote the individual through a decent, secure lifestyle, while at the same time ensuring access to employment, education and culture?

The experience of Lyon illustrates *three key principles* that allow forms of governance to be developed that are adapted to the management of urban disparities:

- *A role of instigator for the State*, which raises the debate about individual responsibilities and defines how action can be taken with regard to direct or indirect financial support.
- *The promotion of local authorities*, essentially at the municipal level, as the focal points around which different parties and services can organise their initiatives on the ground and through which local tensions can be resolved.
- *The need for authorities to function "in tandem"* highlights how: neighbourhood and residents' associations play a leading role; municipal authorities are close to the citizens; metropolitan authorities are the most appropriate level to alleviate urban segregation; other geographically-defined authorities may be involved in the development process.

Involving Residents in Local Decision-making

To develop residents' initiative and to encourage what one might call "self-governance" requires a special effort on the part of the authorities to develop forms of participation that meet the specific expectations of the residents. Such forms of participatory democracy must go beyond the confines of the mere disputed demands or strictly community-based matters.

Urban and Social Work Co-ordination Teams

Creating the actual space for mediation to occur is the specific job of the *Urban and Social Work Co-ordination Teams* which involve professionals in education and other fields. It is the task of these teams to ensure the day-to-day cohesion ("transversality") between the various constituent parts of programmes, to provide the link between the residents' groups and public institutions, and, if necessary, to play the role of mediator between the different communities, social groups and age groups. These teams are delegated by the municipal authorities to take action on particularly sensitive matters such as safety, school performance, cultural development or integration into the economy. Present on the ground, the teams will represent the residents and, in particular, will monitor the results of this participation.

Neighbourhood Councils

The most common form of residents' involvement is to establish *Neighbourhood Councils* or *Committees*. They are made up from representatives of neighbourhood associations and resident volunteers and headed by one elected councillor. These committees meet several times a year to allow residents to express their views on the improvement plans for their neighbourhood, and formulate proposals. Communication specialists are occasionally given a mandate to help residents express their opinions and find a common language between them and the authorities.

Resident Envoys

The *Resident Envoy* initiative has been developed in neighbourhoods where the work of associations has failed. During restoration projects for example, those in charge of the programme seek to involve residents and engage in dialogue with them. A resident volunteer takes responsibility to present the project to his or her neighbours and to convey their reactions to the programme leaders during fairly informal meetings. Co-ordination first relates to the most concrete aspects of the project, and progressively to all aspects of public action and neighbourhood management.

Neighbourhood Corporations

Neighbourhood Corporations are non-profit associations whose aim is to further residents' involvement in improving their environment and developing local services within their neighbourhood. Their objectives are primarily social: re-forging social links in an area blighted by poverty and social exclusion; involving the residents who are most disadvantaged and who have suffered most with unemployment in looking after their urban environment. Corporations pay the residents for temporary full-time or part-time work maintaining the communal parts of buildings and outside spaces, participating in work to make improvements and helping set up new services. Their local contribution is threefold:

- *urban*: they play a role in improving the everyday living environment and the services available;
- *economic*: they redistribute spending power for the benefit of a poor population living in a socially segregated area;
- *social and institutional*: they help to improve the status of everyday tasks by adding a social aspect; they rebuild links between residents; they create a place where people can learn about citizenship and collective values; they are a meeting place between residents and the key players from the local authority in the life of the neighbourhood; above all, they provide a venue for mediation.

The Armstrong Neighbourhood Corporation, for example, employs between 40 and 80 staff every month. It is active in such areas as minor building maintenance, cleaning, maintaining open spaces, removal of litter or debris, building security, supervision of construction work carried out by young people as part of help for those with serious social difficulties. The Armstrong Corporation also played a role in setting up a public crèche, and in supporting cultural and sporting initiatives. Against a difficult social background, it carries on with its long-term work aimed at getting socially and culturally disadvantaged people to eventually assume responsibilities for which they have been neither trained nor initially prepared.

Photo: Agence d'urbanisme, François Guy

Figure 2.4 *"Le Clip de la Cité"*: a social venue in a disadvantaged neighbourhood of Lyon

A Co-ordinating Committee for the Management of Social Venues

The district of Bron to the east of Lyon established a consultation structure for co-ordinating venues used for social purposes in one neighbourhood, after the only venue with the capacity to freely host family meetings, parties or young people's activities was completely vandalised.

Bron's Municipal Council and the Urban Work Co-ordination Team made proposals to the young people and to associations to define new regulations for the community use of social venues. After a consultation period, a *Co-ordination Committee* was created. This is a participatory body presided over by an elected representative of the municipal council, but with the involvement of all users. Internal regulations were set out. This emphasised transparency, rules allowing the widest availability of venues and mutual respect for all in any cases of shared use.

For its part, the municipal council has restored those venues that had been damaged and has re-furnished them. New venues are gradually being made available to the neighbourhood associations or groups that participate in the Co-ordination Committee.

This approach has now been in effect for ten years. Any crises or violent events, when they have recurred, have been overcome. Through the maintained dialogue that this approach has offered between the parties concerned, the whole spirit of the community has changed: the social situation in which people are currently living is now calmer and more conducive to local development initiatives.

The above three examples of participatory involvement are noteworthy because they have lasted a long time and have produced social changes in the neighbourhoods. They may be modest achievements, and they are still fragile. Nevertheless, these neighbourhood projects seem essential within the framework of a participatory, democratic system of local governance. It is in these disadvantaged neighbourhoods that much of Greater Lyon's activity can be found. It is through the capacity to integrate them and to create an open future for them that the conurbation can be best prepared to face the next millennium.

2.6   Recognising New Urban Values for Future Planning

from Geneviève Dubois-Taine, *"About New Urban Values"*

Most planning efforts of the last thirty years have not produced their anticipated impacts. Since the Second World War, planners have usually tried to organise the whole urban area, with mixed activities, medium- and high-density districts and well-defined development areas. However, something very different has happened: sprawling cities with large housing areas of low density, large commercial districts along major roads and non-continuous urban form.

Society today is experiencing major modifications, perhaps as important as during the Renaissance in Europe. The main trends and forces which urban planners previously worked with are little-by-little being replaced by others. Planners have to recognise these new values if efficient policies are to be developed.

What Forces and Values Deeply Modify our Neighbourhoods

To understand how our cities work and are structured, it is necessary to interpret the roles of the different stakeholders that influence them. Not only elected members or urban planners are modelling the city; it is the result of three major categories of stakeholders. It depends on the decisions that people take every day, on their choice of a place of residence, mobility or preferred destination choices, etc. It results from the localisation and activity choices of economic stakeholders. Finally, it is determined by the ambitions and projects of politicians and by the manner in which elected members and planners regulate the different forces in action. Let us look more particularly at the considerations that relate to lifestyles.

First of all, the 20th century has been characterised by a mobility explosion taking many different forms: by car, but also by train, by plane; and more recently wireless communication, telecommunication, mobile phones, etc.

Why is mobility appreciated so much? Mobility allows an experience of the city with a certain richness and a certain anonymity. Mobility allows a sense of multi-belonging and multi-identity. It is quite possible to take roots in different environments, to participate in various activities, to form different identities. Each person chooses to engage in activities in this or that preferred location according to the hour, day, week, month or year. The value attached to the possibility to choose, to be master of one's life strongly emerges from sociological surveys.

The increasing part played by recreational activities in our life is another strong element of the re-composition of neighbourhoods. Let us mention only two aspects of it. The first relates to the new composition of urban rhythms. Instead of a city regulated by the factory clock which used to give a rhythm to urban life, now a multitude of moments are superposed: a 35-hour week, variable timetables, free-choice, part-time,… incite many city dwellers to choose the moments when they take this or that step, engage in recreational activities, or fulfil their social or cultural life. Places and services have drastically been changed by it. Districts which are very specialised time-wise develop beside businesses opened 24 hours a day. The city lives on more and more complex rhythms.

The other aspect is illustrated by the importance of nature in the life of city dwellers. The movement started centuries ago. The English largely made it common-place in the 19th century with their cottages scattered in the countryside. The popularity of individual houses is also one result. But this search for nature also expresses itself in the demand for parks, for nature within the city itself, in the ever increasing number of activities engaged in nature itself. The success of large nature -tourism and -sport operators are there to demonstrated this appeal. It is also expressed in the choice of certain businesses that localise in areas with a strong "countryside" character.

In this context, employment also becomes diversified: jobs in services, modulated in time, distributed in many places, linked with Internet, etc.

In this system, housing appears as the pivot from which one chooses to belong to all those places, and where the various destination locations are selected.

Archipelago Town

A common concept in France is that of the *Archipelago Town* (Viard, 1994; Veltz, 1997), a town made of very many separated *islands*. It is an historical reality: in the Middle Ages, each community had its own street. In many towns, the old names of the streets are still found: Tanners Street, Wheel Street, Shoe Repairers, etc. All these different *islands* and districts exist alongside each other. All have the same value, the same importance: the town centre, the shopping mall, industrial areas, residential districts, etc.

To promote social equity, the essential issue is to connect all the islands together as well as possible — not only the peripheral islands with the centre, but each district with all the other districts. Accessibility through all the parts of the city is one way to promote social equity.

Another issue is to build major infrastructures in some of these *islands*, and not only in the centre. All the population of the city will become used to going everywhere in the urban area. This policy was applied in France where many stadiums were built in districts with social problems. Now multiplex cinemas are built in residential areas with problems, in order to help them develop a new, modern identity.

Further Reading

Begag, A. and Rossini, R. (1999) *"Du bon usage de la distance chez les sauvageons."* Paris: Le Seuil.

Borja, J. (1996) *"Cities:New Roles and Forms of Governing."* In *Preparing for the Urban Future,* edited by M. Cohen et al. Washington: John Hopkins University Press for the Woodrow Wilson Center Press.

Bubba, N. and Lamba, D. (1991) *"Urban Management in Kenya."* *Environment and Urbanization* 3 (1), 37-59.

Campbell, T. (1997) *Innovations and Risk Taking: The Engine of Reform in Local Government in Latin America and the Caribbean.* Washington: World Bank.

Communauté Urbaine de Lyon (2000) *Contrat de ville de l'Agglomération lyonnaise* (document provisoire). Préfecture du Rhône.

Decoutère, S. et al. (eds). (1996) *Le management territorial : pour une prise en compte du territoire dans la nouvelle gestion publique.* Lausanne: PPUR.

Enyedi, Gy. and Pálné Kovács, I. (1994) "The Government and the Local Authorities." In *Balance: The Hungarian Government 1990-1994,* edited by Cs. Gombár, E. Hankiss, L. Lengyel, and Gy. Várnai. Budapest: Korridor.

Enyedi, Gy. (1997) *"Budapest: Return to European Competition."* In *European Cities in Competition,* edited by Ch. Jensen, Buthler, A. Shachar and J. van Weesep. Aldershot: Avebury.

Hirst, T. and Lamba, D. (1994) *The Struggle for Nairobi.* Nairobi: Mazingira Institute.

Lee-Smith, D. and Stren R. (1991) *"New Perspectives on African Urban Management."* *Environment and Urbanization* 3 (1), 23-36.

Maurel E. and Megevand, F. (1996) *La thématique sociale des contrats de ville.* Grenoble, Grefoss.

Mettan, N. and Sfar, D. (1994) *Du conflit à la coopération ou les nouvelles modalités de la gestion des projets urbains: rapport de synthèse*. Zurich and Lausanne: FNRS-PNR 25 and C.E.A.T.

Pálné Kovács, I. (1995) *"The Government's Gestures and Structures in the Process of Decentralization."* In *Question Marks: The Hungarian Government 1994-1995*, edited by Cs. Gombár, E. Hankiss, L. Lengyel, and Gy. Várnai. Budapest: Korridor.

Sivaramakrishnan, K. C. (1996) *"Urban Governance: Changing Realities."* In *Preparing for the Urban Future*, edited by M. Cohen et al. Washington: John Hopkins University Press for the Woodrow Wilson Center Press.

Veltz P. (1997) *Mondialisation villes et territoires: l'économie d'archipel*. Paris: PUF

Viard, J. (1994), *La société d'archipel ou les territoires du village global*. [La Tour d'Aigues]: Editions de l'Aube.

Voisin, B. (1994) *"Repères pour aujourd'hui."* *"Réinterroger les pratiques fondatrices."* *"20 ans de développement social urbain dans l'agglomération lyonnaise."* *Les Cahiers du CR.DSU* 2 (March), Lyon.

Voisin, B. (1999) *"La ville désintégrée ?"*; *"Métropolisation et dynamiques de développement local"*; *"Intervention des habitants et travail social: le quartier Armstrong des Minguettes."* *Hommes et migrations* 1217 (Feb.), Paris.

Voisin, B. (2000) *"Réseaux sociaux et nouvelles formes de vie associative dans les grands ensembles."* *Mémoires et identités de l'agglomération lyonnaise*. Les cahiers Millénaires 3. Grand Lyon prospective 20 (Jan.)

CHAPTER 3

Social and
cultural policies

SOCIAL INTEGRATION AND SPATIAL EQUITY

A particularly important area of urban management is related to social and cultural policies, too often given lower priority than economic and budgetary considerations. This is the case for cities like São Paulo or Nairobi where two social communities live next to each other, one included in the world-system and the other excluded from it. The social structure exists, nonetheless, with its particular mechanisms, its rules and its networks. It enables value to be added to local features and promotes a sense of community. Social institutions, with the support of NGOs, help to integrate those who are, or could become, excluded from urban communities.

When in urban neighbourhoods the role of the family is declining, the sense of community belonging is replaced by functional networks. Social and cultural policies then play a major role in the struggle against social exclusion, and add value to the sense of local identity. Research on immigration in Toronto and Montreal, or on refugee adaptation in Vancouver, indicates avenues for better integration policies.

To favour social and cultural co-operation in the neighbourhoods, urban management can be based on bottom-up approaches (at the neighbourhood level) or top-down policies (at the metropolitan level), but the choice has to be explicitly stated: the options are local strategies to enhance neighbourhood integration, or metropolitan strategies to improve the quality of life and to promote a positive urban vision within a coherent unit. In each case the spatial dimension of policies has to be taken into account; the whole range of stakeholders at the different geographical levels should be involved; and policies have to be devised in terms of social equity and sustainability. Instead of top-down urban management by elected representatives and civil servants, social and cultural policies can be built on the vitality of the local community by involving citizen groups in public life. Innovative ideas on improving street vitality have been tried in Milan, to reduce crime and the sense of insecurity. Such local policies are a driving force for social dynamism and community integration within the urban fabric.

SOCIAL AND ETHNIC DIVERSITY, SAFETY AND URBAN VITALITY

In **Toronto**, research has concentrated on the processes of population redistribution and in particular on the role played by migration and immigration in driving social transformation in Canadian metropolitan areas.

Larry S. Bourne considers immigration as *"one obvious manifestation of globalisation, a major source of social change — as well as a factor in increasing social and ethnic diversity — in many developed countries. But immigration does not take place in a social vacuum. It must be set in the larger context provided by an understanding of population dynamics, and specifically of demographic change and internal migration within the receiving metropolitan areas."*

Research has generally overlooked the study of the processes of population redistribution. *"We know surprisingly little about the geographical distribution of immigrants, their movements after initial settlement and the reasons for their choice of destinations. Nor do we know very much about the relationships between immigration and internal migration, or about the intersection between these two flows and the maintenance of social stability and viability in those urban areas receiving large numbers of domestic and overseas migrants."*

Immigration flows, *"telescoped on a few large metropolitan areas,"* have a significant social impact, which is characterised by a *"rapid transformation of the social landscapes and lifestyles of the population of the entire urban region of several high-immi-*

gration metropolitan areas, and the increasing differentiation of these places from the rest of the country."

The recent immigration/migration experience in the Toronto metropolitan region features several aspects of social change (see Chapter 3.1). It shows that *"with high mobility rates, the potential for the rapid social (and ethno-cultural) transformation of neighbourhoods, indeed of entire urban regions, is very high. A careful monitoring of these trends is an important element in constructing viable social policies."*

Several issues of public policy concern are considered. *As the immigrant population becomes more "distinctive" in terms of ethno-cultural background, language and race, it is reasonable to hypothesise that the spatial dispersion process may well be slower in the future. This question is of fundamental importance for public policy-makers and social service providers. If newer immigrants do not disperse from the gateway centres in the years and decades following their initial arrival, then a different set of policies is necessary to foster their adjustment (or coping) strategies, as well as to assist the receiving cities in meeting the social needs of these immigrants.*

Bourne stresses that *"it is not possible to study either migration or immigration, either as processes of social change, or in terms of their specific social consequences, in isolation. Social sustainability, and the quality of urban life generally, very much depends on how well society responds to the challenges posed by this combination of demographic and migration transitions, and to the resulting increase in the social and ethno-cultural diversity of the resident population."*

In **Montreal**, research has focused on the impact of immigration on the social fabric of cities. Annick Germain stresses that socio-ethnic mix *"becomes a highly sensitive question once the importance of it for the management of social issues, and ultimately for the social sustainability of cities, is realised. Inter-ethnic cohabitation and social cohesion are perhaps thus the two most important issues faced by large cities with growing concentrations of international immigration."*

The author asks who is to address the problem of social exclusion, whether it is a local or a state affair, and if it should be resolved through bottom-up or top-down policies. These questions raise *"the more general issue of the transposition of national policies to the local level and the way in which dynamics specific to this level are taken into account during the conception of policies and programmes."* It is suggested that *"there is a gap that is widening daily between the political agenda which ultimately leads to the creation of governmental policies and programmes, and the dynamics of cohabitation that can be observed at the local level."*

The case of Montreal (see Chapter 3.2), where increasing migratory flows could have generated a significant crisis of social cohesion, illustrates how the issue of multiculturalism can be dealt with and how diversity is experienced in metropolitan multi-ethnic neighbourhoods. The *"dynamic and vibrant social energy"* of these areas is shown to be the *"result of learning how to coexist under conditions of diversity."* The Montreal model, with its ethnic segmentation rather than socio-spatial segregation, *"shows that the utopian idea of residential dispersion is not the only way to achieve relatively non-conflicting inter-ethnic cohabitation."*

Germain concludes that *"one has then to recognise that local and central policies should not necessarily be governed by the same philosophy concerning inter-ethnic cohabitation. A multicultural experience of the city could be a complement to central policies based on integration."*

Another study in **Vancouver** has focused on refugee adaptation by analysing changes in psychological, economic and social factors over the first years of resettlement. Morton Beiser notes that *"during the early years of resettlement, post-migration experience has a more profound effect on mental health than events preceding arrival,"* and suggests that resettlement practices are determinant for refugees to integrate better. *"Receiving societies cannot change the histories of pre-migration trauma and terror that refugees bring with them. They can, however, affect what happens to people after admitting them, a fact that implies both opportunity and responsibility. Good resettlement practices are not only a responsibility, but also an opportunity to help people who require protection to overcome past misfortune and become contributing members of their adopted societies."*

The Vancouver case study (see Chapter 3.3) *"draws on data from the Refugee Resettlement Project, a ten year study of the resettlement and mental health of Southeast Asian refugees in Canada."* It shows *"how the impact of risk and protective factors may change over time. Effective planning must take into*

*account not only programmes that are most likely to be helpful,
but the optimal times to introduce them."*

In **Milan**, a study has been conducted to develop polices on
safety problems in suburban areas. It considers what can be done
to reduce the sense of insecurity, before taking repressive measures. Clara Cardia explains that in Italy, *"the feeling of insecurity
is growing; citizens of large and medium-sized cities pressure
their mayors for more protection, and safety policies have
become a major issue in local government elections."* However,
*"a largely unanswered question is whether the problem of inse-
curity felt by the citizens is directly related to an increase in
crime, or whether it is linked to other societal and urban problems, such as immigration."*

The example of the City of Milan (see Chapter 3.4) shows that
answers will not only be found in the improvement of the physical
urban environment but also in street liveliness or in social mobilisation. Clara Cardia quotes Jane Jacobs (1961, p.31): *"the first
thing to understand is that public peace — the sidewalk and
street peace — of cities is not kept primarily by the police: it is
kept by an intricate, almost unconscious network of voluntary
controls and standards among the people themselves, and
enforced by the people themselves."*

3.1 The Impacts of Domestic Migration and Immigration in Toronto

from Larry S. Bourne, *"Migration, Immigration and Social Sustainability: The Toronto Experience in Comparative Context"*

Spatial Concentration of Immigrants in Metropolitan Areas

Canada has always been a nation of immigration. The present immigrant intake is high, with an annual average of over 220,000 during the 1990s. Immigration is highly concentrated geographically, telescoped on a few metropolitan areas that serve as initial destinations or "gateways"; indeed, the degree of concentration has been increasing over time. As of 1996, 52.4% of all immigrants were resident in the three largest metropolitan areas of Toronto, Montreal and Vancouver. Among recent immigrants (those arriving since 1991), 74% are resident in these three metropolises. One obvious result of this spatial concentration of immigrants is that the level of social differentiation among Canadian urban areas has increased. For all five of the major metropolitan areas, immigration is the largest single component of urban population growth (over 100% in Montreal in the 1990s; 92% in Toronto and 79% in Vancouver).

The origins of immigrants have shifted dramatically over the last two decades to countries that are non-traditional sources, and thus to more culturally and ethnically distinctive populations. In the last decade 70% of immigrants have come from countries in Asia, Africa, the Caribbean and Latin America. The composition of the immigrant population has also shifted in terms of skill levels and resources, and among the three major "classes" of immigrant —family, independent and refugee.

There is also a shift in immigrant populations toward the suburbs, notably the older inner suburbs but more recently to the new suburbs. These are areas where jobs and less expensive housing are more readily available. The traditional immigrant reception areas in the inner cities of urban Canada — although still evident in the landscape — are no longer the primary focus of immigrant destinations. Interestingly, the degree of sub-urbanisation also varies widely among particular immigrant groups. These diverse patterns are partly a reflection of differences in the income and educational levels of the immigrants on arrival, and partly a reflection of the localising effects of chain migrations.

A Dispersed Internal Migration

The overall rate of internal migration in Canada, as in other developed countries, has been remarkably constant over time. Every five years 20.3% of all Canadians move across municipal boundaries. The overall rate is driven primarily by differences in demographic structure and seems to be largely independent of national economic conditions. On the other hand, the actual destinations selected do vary widely from one period to another, depending on regional economic performance as well as which sectors and urban areas are growing or declining. Migration flows within any urban system also tend to be symmetrical, that is in-flows and out-flows are usually of similar magnitude. Net migration flows are thus typically small, but nonetheless significant. Most such net relocations involve movements upward in the urban size hierarchy and outward from the larger metropolitan areas to smaller communities in the periphery of those regions.

The contrast with immigration is obvious: for internal migrants the rate has remained more-or-less constant over time, while the destinations have become more dispersed and more variable from one period to another. Immigration, unlike most domestic migrations, is a more-or-less "managed" flow in the sense that it is subjected to political whims, changes in policy directions, interest-group pressures, and unwritten administrative constraints. The choices of immigrant destinations are typically not based on detailed and current knowledge of the changing economic fortunes of individual places in the urban system, but rather on the locations selected by earlier immigrants of similar ethnic or linguistic background from the same source region or country.

The Recent Toronto Experience

The Greater Toronto Area (GTA) has been the major recipient of *overseas migrants* since World War II, and that proportion has been increasing. The GTA has 37% of all immigrants to Canada, and over 43% of recent immigrants: it is now the most ethnically diverse metropolis on the continent. Most recent immigrants are from non-traditional source countries (South-east Asia, Caribbean).

In parallel with increasing immigration, the Toronto metropolitan area has witnessed a surprisingly sharp reversal of *internal migration* flows. Prior to 1986 Toronto had a relatively balanced migration exchange with other parts of its regional hinterland and with the rest of the country. From 1986 on, in contrast, the net migration balance became negative, and dramatically so. At the same time, foreign immigration accelerated.

Why did this shift happen? The data available indicate that the immigration and migration flows are not statistically independent. As immigration levels increased in the late 1980s and early 1990s, net internal migration became negative. Changes in both in- and out-migration flows contributed to the reversal. In-migration rates for Toronto dropped, while out-migration rates increased.

Where are these people going? Almost everywhere in the country, but especially to the far west, to nearby Oshawa and Hamilton, and to small towns and rural areas in the region around Toronto. These represent different migration flows: those to the west are largely job-related, those to Oshawa and Hamilton are primarily over-spill suburbanisation, while those to small towns likely represent long-distance commuters as well as retirement and recreational migrations.

Migration and immigration flows represent the combined outcomes of housing and labour-market dynamics internal to the region, as well as the push (displacement) and pull (facilitating) effects of higher immigration levels. Higher house prices in metropolitan Toronto in the late 1980s, for example, tended to discourage domestic in-migration while also permitting more equity out-migrants. Higher unemployment levels in the early 1990s also discouraged potential in-migrants, while at the same time encouraging an increase in job-seeking out-migrants.

The migration-immigration relationship, however, is not that simple; public policy and the business cycle have also had an impact. The national recession that began in 1989-90 hit the Toronto regional economy, and its large manufacturing sector, particularly hard. Unemployment rates, formerly among the lowest in the country, reached and then exceeded the national average. Domestic migrants obviously responded to these cues, either by moving out of the metropolitan area or, more often, by not moving in. The flow of immigrants from overseas, in contrast, continued to rise, as permitted by federal government policy. Immigrants, with less explicit information on current economic conditions on which to base their destination choices, came to places in which their kin or countrymen had previously settled. What then appears as a strong inverse time-series correlation between foreign in-migrants and domestic out-migrants in the Toronto case may in fact be, at least in part, an accident of timing with respect to the effects of regional business cycles and public policy decisions.

3.2 Top-down or Bottom-up Immigration Policies in Montreal

from Annick Germain, *"Living with Cultural and Ethnic Diversity: An Urban Affair. The case of Montreal"*

Immigration: A Long Tradition and a Recent Issue of Local Concern

Quebec has very high rates of international immigration (25,000 to 30,000 immigrants on average each year); 88% of these immigrants live within the greater Montreal area (3.3 million residents). The Montreal area, however, has proportionally fewer immigrants than the other two main Canadian metropolises (17.8% in Montreal; 34.9% in Vancouver and 41.9% in Toronto). On the other hand, Montreal has a very diversified pattern of immigration: since the mid-1970s, immigration from developing countries has overtaken that from Europe, and this ethnic diversity can be seen throughout the city and in its neighbourhoods.

Another characteristic is that Montreal is a "divided" city, long torn between dual majorities: the English majority which held economic power and the French majority which had the benefit of population size and controlled most provincial political institutions. Montreal was strongly segmented both ethno-culturally and linguistically, and the concept of "mosaic" then seemed to apply well before international immigration even became an issue.

Immigration in Quebec is almost exclusively a metropolitan issue. Paradoxically, until the 1990s, the local authorities have not taken much interest in this. Perhaps due in part to its shared federal-provincial jurisdiction, immigration has only recently been seen as an issue that concerns municipal actors, and that justifies examination through the lens of urban planning.

A Local or State Affair?

A certain degree of centralisation is evident in immigration policies, even though the provincial government has had considerable powers of intervention in immigrant selection, settlement, and integration programmes since the 1970s (control over expenses relating to immigrant reception and settlement; selection of independent and business-class immigrants; selection of immigrants in the family and refugee classes).

Many federal and provincial immigration programmes are currently administered in partnership with certain NGOs active in immigrant reception and settlement. The sizeable devolution of programme management to NGOs and community associations is partly the result of government downsizing and pressure from the grassroots level. As "programme managing agencies," these associative and community networks are required to comply with federal and provincial frameworks and directives, which can alter their modes of operation in the long run.

There is a gap between the political agenda and the dynamics of cohabitation that can be observed at the local scale. In other words, the multi-ethnic Montreal of today seems to be fed by diverging perceptions which divide Montrealers between political norms and debates and the lived spaces of daily life.

Citizen or City Dweller?

Owing to the awareness of the danger represented by anglicised immigrants, the control of immigration became an important issue for Quebec. An accord was negotiated with the federal government in the 70s to give the province full power over the selection of economic immigrants (independent and business immigrants). Simultaneously, the federal government launched its policy of multiculturalism, which made the recognition of cultural diversity one of the main pillars of the Canadian State.

Quebec's official discourse evolved rather quickly. The concept of *intercultural relations* was advanced to highlight interchange between cultures, but also to make integration the ultimate goal of immigrant insertion in the host society. However, this is not a matter of espousing an assimilation model to guarantee social cohesion. Successive policy announcements have delineated the *moral contract* between the immigrants and the receiving society; the *common public culture* on which a plural Quebec must be based; and most recently the notion of *citizenship*. This latter notion is not necessarily well received in Quebec by cultural minorities, especially when the government which promotes it is also extolling independence. Was this an attempt to challenge the newly pluralist Quebec? The abandonment of the notion of "cultural community" in Quebec's governmental discourse worries ethno-cultural minorities who do not necessarily see that multiculturalism can have particular resonance in a society where, not too long ago, the French speaking majority had the impression of being a minority in its own constituency. This debate is particularly sensitive at a time when the nationalist movement is questioning the foundation of its identity: is it based on territory or ethnicity? Once more, the question of immigration becomes highly charged in a context where the host society itself fears its own fragmentation.

Relative Concentration of Immigrants in the Montréal CMA in 1996,
by Census Tract, for All Countries and Regions

Location Quotient

☐   0 - 0.5   (233)
▨   0.5 - 1.4 (317)
▩   1.5 - 2.4 (156)
■   2.5 - 3.7 (50)
⠿   Uninhabited
     or no data

0 ____ 10 Km

Cartographie INRS-Urbanisation, 1998

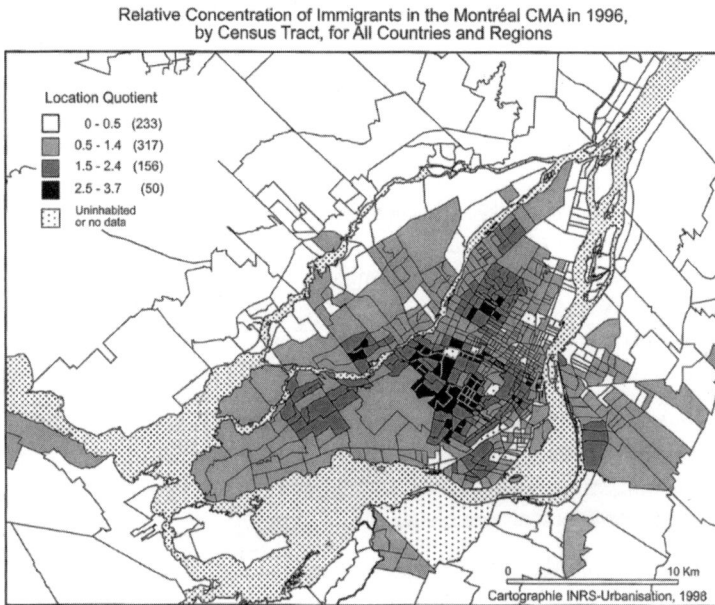

Figure 3.1 **Relative Concentration of Immigrants in the Montreal Census Metropolitan Area in 1996** *(by census tracts, for all counties and regions)*

Everyday Multiculturalism vs. Integration

Montreal's urban life reveals a lifestyle in which a form of everyday multiculturalism prevails (see Figure 3.1). Eating establishments, groceries and places of worship, often important places of hospitality for new immigrants, dot the symbolic landscape of many neighbourhoods.

Public spaces are the scene of great ethnic diversity, in which coexistence is peaceful but where little mixing between different cultures occurs. The exception is children and youth, who mix voluntarily. In these spaces, residents share an urban code which urges them to keep their distance, while taking pleasure from being in the midst of such a society.

Multi-ethnic neighbourhoods are charged with dynamic and vibrant social energy. The ethnic diversity of neighbourhoods is considered by many residents as a "cultural comfort." This suspends their status as minorities in the space-time of neighbourhood life, where everyone is first and foremost a city dweller. However, this feeling is not spontaneous; it is the result of learning how to coexist under conditions of diversity.

The most successful cosmopolitan neighbourhoods seem to be those that offer a vast panoply of sites that are sometimes the preserve of specific groups and sometimes more open to diversity. One must be first able to find oneself among one's own, but in principle and in practice one must also be able to enter public spaces which are open to everyone.

The experience of the city is a crucial step in the process of integration because of its specific character — a degree of multiculturalism combined with urbanity which permits communication despite the distance in-between. This way of "being together" contrasts with provincial government policies which condemn multiculturalism and exalt the community model.

One has then to recognise that local and central policies should not necessarily be governed by the same philosophy concerning inter-ethnic cohabitation. A multicultural experience of the city could be a complement to central policies based on integration.

Ethnic segmentation (as opposed to socio-spatial segregation) is an integral part of the Montreal model, and shows that the utopian idea of residential dispersion is not the only way to achieve relatively non-conflicting inter-ethnic cohabitation.

The multi-ethnic areas are at the same time made up of poor neighbourhoods at the centre of the agglomeration and of affluent suburbs, as well as a whole gamut of intermediate situations. A progressive spreading of immigration occurs, while a division of space exists along ethnic lines. Public authorities have only rarely intervened in immigrant's urban localisation patterns. Specifically, they acted in the case of particular refugee groups. Generally where one lives is a choice available to all individuals. Therefore, accessibility is after all a better goal for policies than is social mix.

3.3   Refugee Resettlement and Adaptation in Vancouver

from Morton Beiser, *"Language Acquisition, Employment and Mental Health Among Southeast Asian Refugees: A Ten-year Study"*

A Psychological, Economic and Social Study

In 1981, the Centre for Addiction and Mental Health at the Department of Psychiatry of the University of Toronto, began a longitudinal study of the psychological, economic and social adaptation of South Asian survivors of war, persecution, flight and refugee camp internment.

Changes in putative risk and protective factors were examined at three different periods (*wave 1*: 1981; *wave 2*: 1983; *wave 3*: 1991) during the first decade of the refugees' life in Vancouver, as well as their respective mental health effects at each point in time.

The following *specific hypotheses* were investigated:
- throughout the resettlement period, unemployment is both a contemporaneous and predictive risk factor for depression;
- English fluency is a contemporaneous and predictive mental health protective factor;
- depression has a feedback effect on both employment and English-speaking ability;
- language facility increases the likelihood of being employed;
- associations between age, gender, education and depression are mediated by the effects of employment and education; if elderly refugees appear to be at higher risk for depression than the younger, the greater likelihood that young refugees will be working and speaking the host country language should explain this association.

Over the ten-year period, the following changes in mental health, employment, and language fluency were identified:
- the prevalence of major depression declined;
- labour force participation increased;
- the unemployment level first increased, then decreased;
- in 1991, the unemployment rate of the sample was 8.1% (9.9% in the Province of British Columbia);
- the passage of time was accompanied by increased levels of English-language proficiency.

Psychological, Economic and Social Adaptation of Refugees

Mental Health

Southeast Asian refugees were displaying remarkably good psychological and economic adaptation a decade after they first arrived in Canada (see Figure 3.2). During the first two years, rates of depression amongst refugees approximated those found in majority culture North American communities. Thereafter, the prevalence of depression declined; after a decade, it was far lower than the rates found in most general population surveys. Selection factors help explain what appear to be counter-intuitive findings: Canadian immigration officers working in the refugee camps of Southeast Asia screened applicants carefully in order to select those most likely to adapt successfully in Canada.

Employment

The decline in unemployment (see Figure 3.2) probably helps explain the improvement in refugee mental health over time. Ten years after they arrived in Canada, the refugees were more likely than resident Canadians to be working. Although unemployment rates among refugees at *wave 3* were low, the mental health salience of unemployment was stronger at this point than at earlier stages of resettlement. *Wave 1* unemployment exerted some predictive effect on *wave 3* unemployment, indicating partly that refugees who were not working after ten years were becoming part of a chronically unemployed, poor and psychologically depressed underclass.

The emergence of unemployment as a risk factor for depression only after the refugees had been in Canada for about two years is consistent with findings reported in another study. During the first two years that the refugees were in Canada, unemployment affected their mental health only because it created economic deprivation, and not, as it does in majority culture populations, owing to stigmatisation and social isolation. Although unemployment may have been relatively non-stressful and expected during the initial period of resettlement, refugees who were not working at the end of ten years felt out of step, not only with majority culture norms, but with the over-all success of their fellow refugees.

At *wave 1*, young refugees experienced a greater risk for depression than their older counterparts. Over time, however, the mental health advantage of age disappeared, probably because the reduced likelihood of employment or of achieving linguistic fluency balanced off any initial mental health advantages otherwise enjoyed by older persons.

Rates of Depression 1981-1991

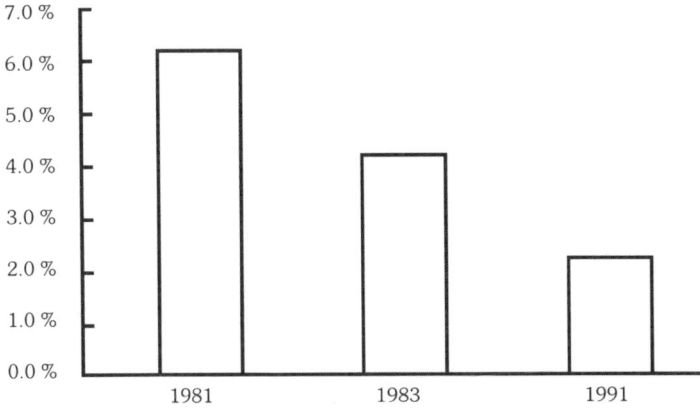

Labour Force Activities 1981-1991

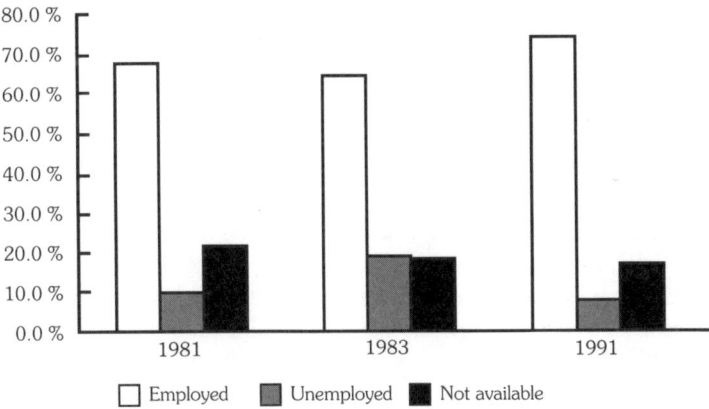

☐ Employed   ■ Unemployed   ■ Not available

English-language Ability 1981-1991

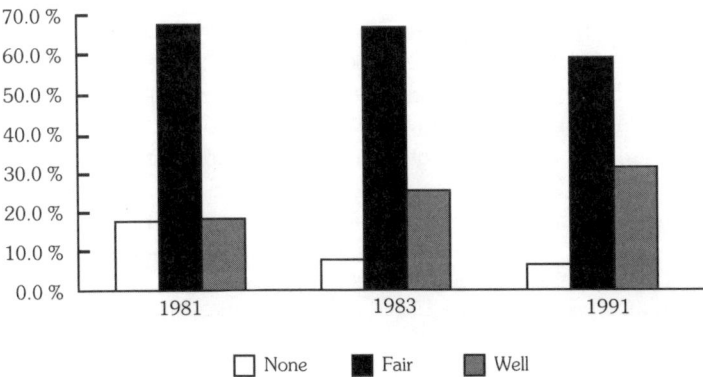

☐ None   ■ Fair   ■ Well

Figure 3.2 **Refugee Psychological, Economic and Social Adaptation:** *Changes in mental health, employment levels and English-language ability*

Language

As a group, the refugees showed steady progress in acquiring English (see Figure 3.2). However, the small core who spoke no English even after a decade in Canada are a source of potential concern. According to the data in this report, although linguistic ability did not compromise employability during the initial years of resettlement, it did affect the chances of working during later years. During their first few years in the country, the refugees tended to work at menial jobs where linguistic fluency probably made little difference. However, as the years went by, their occupational status tended to increase and language probably became an important factor in determining occupational mobility.

Aside from its effect on employability, lack of language also compromises access to services and limits options to participate in other important domains, such as civic life and main-stream entertainment. It is particularly troubling that precisely those persons most likely to be isolated by circumstance — women, the poorly educated and the elderly — are those least likely to learn English, and thus to risk further isolation.

Social Policy Implications

The study findings highlight the importance of a dynamic resettlement model, one that allows for the possibility that the salience of risk and protective factors changes over time. Mental health during the initial periods of resettlement affects subsequent adaptation. The early identification and treatment of psychiatric problems would potentially benefit future mental health as well as socio-economic adjustment. Although refugees may avoid "mainstream" mental health services, they will use and benefit from culturally sensitive care.

These findings serve to focus attention on what happens to people as they go about trying to resettle in a new country, a period during which the policies and programmes of receiving societies can potentially make a large difference in the lives of the uprooted and dispossessed. Resettlement is a long-term process, and post-migration factors may have different mental health effects at different stages in the resettlement process. Planners must be sensitive to this principle in order to develop programmes that will meet the changing needs of refugees as they confront the changing challenges of resettlement.

3.4   Social and Spatial Policies for a Safer City of Milan

from Clara Cardia, *"Vitality and Safety: A Project for the Milan Urban Fringe"*

A Project Linking Quality of Life and Safety

The problem of insecurity has recently encouraged the City of Milan to develop a special project for safety, entitled *"Quality of Life and Safety in Milan,"* which clearly expresses its approach. The project is aimed at promoting actions that will diminish the amount of petty crime in the city, and reduce the citizens' sense of insecurity and fear of crime.

The overall philosophy of the project is that, in order to maintain or rebuild a safe urban environment, action has to focus on social and environmental factors as well as on law enforcement. Law enforcement often obtains immediate results, whereas social and environmental actions produce long-lasting results.

In order to achieve this, an agreement of co-operation has been signed by the Mayor of the City, and the Chief of Police. The *Quality of Life and Safety Project* has a "Special Project" status. It is overseen by the Milan Local Government Administration, with a director, a small staff, and special funding. Its activity is supported by a scientific committee composed of experts in the fields of planning, health, criminology and sociology. Its role is to assist the "young" project structure in building up long-term strategies as well as immediate short-term actions.

The "Zone 17" Pilot Area Study

The "Zone 17 Pilot Area Study" is included within the overall city strategy for safety. It explores methods for maintaining, or restoring, a safe urban environment. First, the study deals with prevention rather than improving a highly degraded environment. Second, it deals with a large urban area of the city, rather than being limited to a small-scale, neighbourhood or few blocks- action.

The study area is 7 square km and has a population of 80,000. Its social composition is mainly middle class, with some upper class housing estates and some degrading public housing estates. The most striking problem of the area is its lack of vitality: parks are not used; high-rise buildings are surrounded by fenced areas; commercial activities are scarce or closed, cafés shut at sunset. The result is a very low level of street life.

An Environmental Approach to Revitalising Public Spaces

The study focuses on the environmental aspects of urban safety. The "environmental approach" considers that the *physical quality* of the environment can help to reduce crime in a neighbourhood.

This concept also includes the *mobilisation of the local community*. It helps the community to regard the future positively, while creating opportunities to meet, generating practical actions such as teaching people to be watchful, promoting volunteer patrols, etc.

The environmental approach can finally be extended to a third field, which is the *revitalisation of public spaces*. This approach is particularly relevant in a Mediterranean culture, where the use of urban spaces has always been central to social interaction.

Action to improve safety should bear on three features:
- *design and maintenance* of spaces (modifying entrances, fences, bus stops, greenery, improving lighting, cleanliness, care);
- promotion of *street vitality* (acting on commercial activities, opening hours, use of ground floors, transportation, promotion of social, cultural, recreational activities, etc.);
- *mobilisation of social groups* to prevent crime (increasing informal control, promoting stronger neighbourhood ties, strengthening the sense of belonging).

The study consisted first in developing a method for the evaluation of safety in the study area in environmental terms. Maps were produced, which define five degrees of "environmental safety" for all the streets and public spaces in the study area during day and night. Second, the study has focused on people's perception of safe and unsafe places in their community. More than 700 interviews were carried out with ordinary street users, and their results have been transferred to maps (see Figure 3.3).

The "Security Grid"

Main streets tend to cumulate more factors promoting environmental safety than secondary and local streets. In some parts of the city, main streets form a continuous primary grid of safe paths, which have been called the "Security Grid." People on this grid can walk in environmentally safe terms by day and by night.

In terms of strategy, the Security Grid means:
- supporting a strong and continuous *primary grid*, where vitality, together with other environmental protection factors and police, will create a lively and safe environment during the day and at night;
- developing a *secondary grid* where safety is supported by other factors, such as good architectural features, lack of visual obstacles, lighting, informal control by residents, community patrolling, guardians or doormen, electronic devices, etc.

Source: City of Milan, Laboratorio Qualità Urbana, 1998

Figure 3.3 **Environmental Safety in Milan:** extract of the plan "Safety in Public
Spaces at Night" showing five degrees of perceived safety in the streets
and parks of the study area (secure, sufficiently secure, quite secure, not
quite secure, not secure)

The following types of action could be carried out to *reinforce the
grid*: to extend opening hours of cafes and shops in key locations; to
encourage cultural and recreational activities to move to ground floors;
to create a young people's centre in an empty school building; to
improve the physical environment (such as greenery, lighting, maintenance, etc.)

The next stage will hopefully be to work with local partners on
implementation. This is quite a challenge, as Milan has no experience
of this type of work. Who would run the project, how would it be
financed, how would the concerned local government agencies be
involved?

Further Reading

Beiser, M. (1999) *Strangers at the Gate: The "Boat People's" First Ten Years in Canada*. Toronto: University of Toronto Press.

Beiser, M., Gill, K. and Edwards R. G. (1993) *"Mental Health Care in Canada: Is It Accessible and Equal?"* Canada's Mental Health 41, 2-7.

Bourne, L.S. and Ley, D. (eds.) (1993) *"The Changing Social Geography of Canadian Cities."* Montreal: McGill-Queens University Press.

Frey, W. and Liaw, K.-L. (1998) *"Immigrant Concentration and Domestic Migrant Dispersal."* Professional Geographer 50 (2), 215-232.

Frisken, F. (ed.) (1994) *"The Changing Canadian Metropolis: A Public Policy Perspective."* Berkeley: University of California, Institute of Government Studies Press.

Germain, A., Blanc, B., Charbonneau, J., Dansereau, F. and Rose, D. (1995) *"Cohabitation inter-ethnique et vie de quartier"*. Gouvernement du Québec, Ministère des affaires internationales, des communautés culturelles et de l'immigration. Études et documents 12.

Helly, D. (1996) *"Le Québec face à la pluralité culturelle."* 1997-1994. *"Un bilan documentaire des politiques."* Sainte-Foy: Institut québécois de recherches sur la culture/Presses de l'Université Laval.

Murdie, R. (1998) *"The Welfare State, Economic Restructuring and Immigrant Flows: Impacts on Socio-Spatial Segregation in Greater Toronto."* In *Urban Segregation and the Welfare State: Inequality and Exclusion in Western Cities*, edited by S. Musterd and W. Ostendorf. London: Routledge.

Pietrantonio, L., Juteau, D. and McAndrew M. (1996) *"Multiculturalisme ou intégration: un faux débat."* In *Les convergences culturelles dans les sociétés pluriethniques*, edited by K. Fall, R. Hadj-Moussa, D. Simeoni. Montréal: Presses de l'Université du Québec.

CHAPTER 4

Public services

MANAGING PUBLIC SERVICES

The smooth running of public services is another key element in the quality of urban life: not only does it contribute to the attractiveness of cities, but it also generates economic impacts. The provision of good services and efficient infrastructure favours the development of the private sector and reduces running costs. In many cities, however, public services have not been designed to improve the quality of life but to solve problems — such as sanitation, traffic control, household refuse disposal, etc. — as they occur.

At a time when municipal management is facing major financial pressures, local authorities are confronted with growing demands from citizens and economic stakeholders. The challenge for the public sector is a difficult one: ensuring quality service provision according to precise criteria, with fewer and fewer resources. When these services do not meet quality standards, then the legitimacy of a local authority is questioned.

"To do more with less" or "to act differently" are key elements of the challenge facing many cities, Geneva, Montreal or Budapest alike. From a free-market point of view, public services should be run as a private business. However, their mission is often not profitable, and viable services such as refuse collection or water supply must be split from those that cannot be profitable. Reorganisation is necessary for competitively run public enterprises; for those that are not, their organisational mission and relevance ought to be rethought. Such is the case for health, education and social services.

Policies to improve public services can also be built on the vitality of the local community by involving citizen groups in public life: such approaches have been tried in Cape Town's shanty towns, in order to improve sanitation and housing conditions.

To ensure quality public services, some cities have had to identify priority areas for action, then anticipate results and the financial resources required. Contracts have been signed with the private sector. In other cases, the notion of public services has remained associated with municipal tasks but with a more dynamic vision than in the past: efficiency, flexibility, organisational coherence, creative ability are elements of this difficult value-added objective. Only rarely have cities not considered the privatisation of certain services, especially water supply, the provision of electricity and refuse collection. This solution, however, is not applicable to health and social services, especially in economically deprived urban areas.

SOCIAL EXCLUSION AND METROPOLITAN INTEGRATION

Throughout **Nairobi**'s history, failure to extend basic services to deprived neighbourhoods has resulted in a form of social exclusion (see Chapter 4.1). Diana Lee-Smith and Davinder Lamba describe how public policy intentions about service provision have not been implemented. Today, large areas of informal settlements with a substantial population are still largely unserviced.

In recent years, the processes of confrontation and civic organisation have constituted significant cases of public pressure for change. Slum dwellers are taking matters into their own hands, getting support from NGOs and organising themselves into lobby associations to improve basic services delivery.

In **Budapest,** the lack of metropolitan co-operation between the capital city and its region has had significant impacts on the quality of public service provision and effectiveness (see Chapter 4.2). Richard Ongjerth notes that, owing to *"the organisational system of public administration, as well as the lack of voluntary communication and co-operation, governing and planning might be termed as rather fragmented, less co-ordinated. This naturally has its impact on the development quality of the region and also on the efficiency of intended development."* As a direct consequence, Budapest has had to consider whether to privatise or to strengthen public services. Autonomous solutions prove to be inadequate, indicating that service provision needs to be better integrated within the framework of a regional policy.

In **Cape Town**, as other cites in South Africa, the situation in respect of services in the aftermath of apartheid is disastrous, with a large population living in informal settlements without adequate water and sanitation. A subsidy-based housing and infrastructure programme for the poor was chosen by the new democratic government to address this issue. John Abbott describes how, despite the completion of a very significant number of houses, the housing backlog has increased. And those who are allocated a new house can not afford to pay for services. *"As with other countries with high rates of urban growth, South Africa is slowly discovering that the only long-term solution to the housing crisis is to embark on a programme of informal settlement upgrading."*

An study was embarked upon to develop a replicable methodology for up-grading informal housing (see Chapter 4.3). It was followed by a pilot project in a settlement of Cape Town with 3000 families, aiming for a substantial densification of the site.

The approach to sustainability of services for this project has been that *"if people are to be able to stay in the settlement after upgrading, the issue of affordability has to be dealt with at the planning stage, not at the stage of the occupation of houses and the delivery of the first services account."* Four sustainability components are at the basis of this approach — one social, one economic, one technical and one organisational. A geographical information system (GIS) system has been established to manage the upgrading project — to map social data, make linked analysis of a wide range of indicators, process all information pertaining to the infrastructure — which constitutes *"only a small step to creating an asset management system and a maintenance programme."*

4.1   Servicing Land: A Dimension of Social Transformation in Nairobi

from Diana Lee-Smith and Davinder Lamba, *"Social Transformation in a Post-Colonial City: The Case of Nairobi"*

Social Exclusion in Non-Serviced Areas

The availability of land, for housing, agricultural production or business, is the most basic resource in a city. It is through restricting access to it that the Nairobi authorities have practised social exclusion, racially in the colonial city and economically in the post-colonial city. The servicing of land is another dimension of social exclusion which was practised in both eras of Nairobi's development, namely, through the failure to extend services to areas inhabited by the excluded group.

These practices date back to *the earliest days of the colonial city.* At the beginning of the century, African housing inside the boundary was banned, except in a small area to the east. People therefore settled outside the boundaries, and these are some of today's informal settlements. African housing areas that grew up inside the boundary were demolished and residents were evicted. In 1919, an official African housing area was designated, but people had to build their housing themselves and no services were provided. More such areas were designated later. Whereas Europeans were given freehold titles to land, Africans were only allowed usufruct rights, meaning they could not buy or sell the property.

The first city council housing for Africans was built in 1921, as a barrack-type dormitory for returning soldiers. Until independence in 1963, more working-class African housing estates were built along the railway line to the east of the town centre. Unauthorised settlements continued to be demolished and peripheral settlements grew. Access to the urban area was then also strictly controlled through a pass system. Today, these same areas house substantial numbers of Nairobi residents, and are still largely unserviced.

After independence, policy intentions to house Nairobi's population were not implemented. In the 1960s, a United Nations study outlined an approach to providing serviced sites to meet the growing need of the urban population for affordable housing. However, by the late 1970s only 6,000 units had been built, falling far short of demand. As a result, the amount of informal housing grew at an even faster rate. In 1971 it was estimated that one-third of the city's population was living in unauthorised housing.

Evictions occurred in the late 1960s and early 1970s, and again in late 1978, when many people were driven out of informal settlements in middle-income neighbourhoods and the city centre and moved to the east of Mathare Valley. Thus the pattern of social exclusion in the eastern unserviced areas was repeated with a vengeance by the post-colonial city authorities.

Today, although the average density in Nairobi is 2,200 persons per square kilometre, densities are up to 40-50,000 persons per square kilometre in some informal settlements (see Figure 4.1). Not less then 55% of the population lives on 5.8% of the residential land, and these densely settled informal areas are virtually denied access to services.

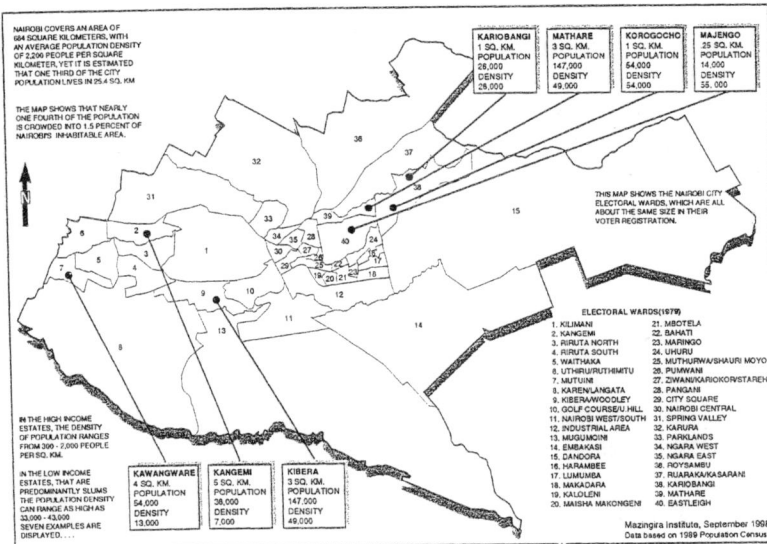

Source: Polèse and Stren (2000)

Figure 4.1 **Population Density and Social Disparity in Nairobi:** an important part of the most crowded and poorest residential areas are deprived of basic services

Corruption, Confrontation and Civic Organisation

Nonetheless, the authorities are involved in the creation and management of the informal settlements through the local chiefs and district administration. People are settled on public land by the administration, and representatives of the administration sit on their local committees. Owing to the informal nature of the settlements, the process has become corrupted, with officials requiring bribes — *kitu kidogo*, meaning something small — for each plot.

This custom creates its own form of business; unscrupulous people buy public land from these officials and become slumlords, building wooden or mud-and-wattle structures which are then rented out to the poor as housing or business premises or both. In one settlement it was found that 87% of residents were tenants. The landlords range from politicians to local residents. The chiefs, supported by the village committees, the administration police, and gangs of youth attached to the ruling political party, act as enforcers.

As political pressure for reform and multiparty democracy mounted in the 1990s, forced evictions of people from their homes and places of work have become even more prevalent, but they have also been met with more resistance, in terms of both physical confrontation and organisation. Violent evictions of residents and informal-sector businesses have occurred in the city centre and suburbs, affecting tens of thousands of people and sometimes accompanied by running street battles. Many evictions are precipitated by the phenomenon of "land grabbing" whereby the "private developer" connives with city authorities or provincial administration to clear plots, most of which are in fact on public land.

The slum dwellers are increasingly taking matters into their own hands, battling those who attempt to encroach on their land, to destroy their shelters and put up fencing or permanent structures. At the same time, they are getting legal support from NGOs and organising themselves into an advocacy organisation, *Muungano wa Wanavijiji Maskini*, with a membership from 86 communities in Nairobi and its environs. Mob justice got the upper hand, when three security guards from a team sent to demolish the slum were lynched. A number of cases have been taken to court; however, there have been no court rulings in favour of low-income people. Middle-income neighbourhoods have also taken the initiative to organise associations that can deliver services or lobby with the authorities on behalf of their members.

4.2   Public Services and Regional Co-operation in Budapest

from Richard Ongjerth, "Governing and Planning Issues of Budapest Region"

Public Institutions: An Efficient Regional Co-operation

With respect to public institutions (education, health care, public security, etc.) co-operation between Budapest and its region has already existed for several decades.

Budapest is in a substantially better position than smaller settlements: certain services of the capital — such as secondary schools or hospitals — exceed the basic requirements. For a long time these services in Budapest have accepted students and patients from the city's hinterland. For practical reasons, the Metropolitan Municipality has also established its living-in social or health-care institutions in other settlements of the region, or in settlements in other parts of the country, occasionally at distances exceeding 100 kilometres. In recent years reciprocity has emerged. Certain private schools in settlements in the Budapest region receive increasing numbers of students from the capital.

Public Utilities: Uncoordinated Action and Local Disparities

The situation is different in relation to public utilities, as these are essentially tied to location and typically serve a settlement.

Budapest operates separate companies, some partly privatised, to provide communal type services (water supply, sewage treatment, gas supply, maintenance of public grounds). The situation is much more heterogeneous in the region. Several communal services firms operate in different settlements or parts of the Pest County. Other settlements have established organisations providing local services, particularly for water supply and sewage treatment. Occasionally two or more local authorities co-operate.

The development of rather under-developed public utilities in the region was — and still is today — of particular importance both at the local and governmental levels of development policy. All these locally operated public utilities have however resulted in rather complex, difficult to oversee and often irrational solutions in the field of communal services. Sometimes it has also resulted in extremely varied service charges. For example, in a newly seweraged dormitory settlement, water and sewerage charges are about ten times higher than in Budapest.

Water Supply

The majority of settlements are not purchasing the — at present — cheaper water from Budapest because they are afraid of becoming dependent. Instead, by striving to attain autarchy, they are choosing more expensive solutions.

Waste Water Treatment

With respect to waste water treatment the problem appears different as even Budapest has insufficient treatment capacity: currently about one quarter of its sewage is treated biologically. The situation is also not satisfactory in the outskirts of the city. In recent years suburban settlements have built waste water treatment plants one after the other, and in certain cases by joining resources. However, when one of the outer districts of Budapest wanted to pipe its sewage to the treatment plant of the neighbouring city with excess capacity, the effort was stopped by the Metropolitan Municipality.

Domestic Waste Disposal

Co-operation is also lacking in the field of waste disposal. Budapest in itself has inadequate capacity for waste recycling or dumping. Therefore part of the communal waste generated is dumped outside the city — in the agglomeration or in more remote settlements. Waste management in the settlements of the region can also be termed as very deficient. In most of the villages, garbage is simply transported to the local dump site which often does not meet even the most elementary environmental protection conditions. In this situation, collaboration by municipalities around the capital has occurred sometimes to install a common waste disposal site. This is also encouraged by the system of state subsidies. However, Budapest usually comes to an agreement only with those local authorities which are of interest to the capital. Wider co-operation with the participation of Budapest is not common.

4.3   Upgrading Informal Settlements in Cape Town

from John Abbott, *"Servicing Informal Settlements: A Case Study From South Africa"*

When South Africa's first democratic government was elected in 1994, it was faced with a disastrous situation in respect of housing and services. Over 1M families were living in informal settlements (which accounted for approximately 17% of the urban population) while an equal number lived in backyard shacks or sub-standard accommodation (Central statistical service of the South African Government. Results calculated from the 1996 census). The majority of these families also lacked access to safe water supplies and water-borne sewerage. This crisis was accompanied by a situation where there were high levels of default on service payments, arising from a policy of opposition to apartheid.

The method that the new government chose to address these issues was a subsidy-based housing and infrastructure programme for the poor. A capital subsidy was provided to each person allocated a new site for a house, which was intended to cover the cost of physical infrastructure and a basic core house (of approximately 25m^2). The government then set a target of building one million houses in its first term of office.

Photo: Department of Civil Engineering, University of Cape Town

Figure 4.2 **Shacks on Illegally-occupied Land in New Rest, Cape Town**

By the end of the term, the government had completed 750 000 houses. However, the housing backlog had increased to 3-4 millions, with the majority of those in poor housing still being without adequate water and sanitation. While a concerted drive to encourage payment for services had been partially successful, the majority of those moving to the new houses were still not paying for services, although in this case the reason was primarily financial rather than political. The majority of people could not afford this level of services.

Today, there is still a 3.7 million houses backlog (Business Day newspaper, 24 February 2000). The majority of the new homeless live in informal settlements, that is shacks of low-quality materials constructed on land which has been illegally occupied (see Figure 4.2). As with other countries with high rates of urban growth, South Africa is slowly discovering that the only long-term solution to the housing crisis is to embark on a programme of informal settlement upgrading. However, although there have been a number of such schemes in Durban and Johannesburg, there is still little understanding of how this process works.

In 1996, the Department of Civil Engineering at the University of Cape Town embarked upon an informal settlement upgrading study which was intended to develop a replicable methodology for upgrading. In January 1999, the methodology was initiated in a pilot project with 3000 families in New Rest (Cape Town). This required that all families had a secure piece of land, with a major road access network. This in turn required that the density be increased from 70 dwellings per hectare (due to the informal nature of the site the gross density was also, effectively, the net density) to approximately 100 dwellings per hectare net, a substantial densification (see Figure 4.3).

A detailed social and economic survey of residents indicated that 59.2% worked in the formal sector, 22.6% in the informal sector, and 19.2% had no recognised form of income. If people are to be able to stay in this settlement after upgrading, then the issue of affordability has to be dealt with at the planning stage, not at the stage of the occupation of houses and the delivery of the first services account. This is the approach taken here.

The approach to sustainability of services for this project has four components, one social, one economic, one technical and one organisational. Each of these is discussed below.

Social Sustainability

The project employs a full time social worker with a staff of five community development workers to support community processes. The support has a number of different roles.

Photo: DAEL, Geneva

Figure 4.3 **Up-graded Housing in New Rest, Cape Town**

- *Information sharing.* Given that the team work at a one on one level, they provide an effective mechanism for explaining the process and ensuring that all families know what is happening and how to contribute. In this regard the team is able to ensure that all residents understand the full financial implications attached to the provision of services, as well as the concept of levels of service
- They provide a *support focus aimed at those lacking any form of income.* The social and economic survey is linked by a GIS database to shack numbers and head of households. This allows the social data to be mapped, as well as providing the basis for linked analysis of a wide range of indicators.

  In the first instance all those who stated that they lack income are approached by the social team. The first step is to identify whether or not their circumstances have changed since the survey. If not then their individual circumstances are quantified. This information can be correlated with other data (e.g. single parent, skills) to provide profiles of the households. This has two objectives. The first is to explore potential economic options for the households. The second in to stimulate debate on levels of service.
- They ensure that *no households is marginalised* from the process because of their circumstances. Since 50% of households are headed by females, and the majority are single parent families, this provides a crucial means of ensuring that those women who are unable to attend meetings can still play an equal role in decision-making.
- They provide *a crucial outlet* for people to discuss their personal problems. While this was not the original intent, the success of the project cannot be separated from these personal issues, particularly in this environment. The outcome of this activity has been the establishment of a joint committee, including the University, Council and Community, to find ways of integrating informal settlement residents more directly into the social infrastructure framework of the city.

Economic Indicators and Programmes

The economic analysis divides the population into those that have formal employment, those working in the informal sector, and those without paid income. Given that economic activity is perceived to be one of the keys to sustainability, the project focuses on supporting and developing this activity area. The project focuses primarily on those working in the informal sector and those without employment. South Africa is fortunate in having a housing subsidy scheme which provides a capital injection into the project at the beginning. To date this has not been used particularly well to support communities. In this project, however, the intent is to maximise the amount of this subsidy that can be spent within the community. Thus all construction is labour-based, while supervision costs are minimised and large contractors are not involved. The survey identified the level of skills within the community and this will be used to match skills to employment opportunities.

Construction raises opportunities not only for labour, but also for the supply of goods and services. External funding has been raised to support the development of small businesses aligned to the construction activities of infrastructure and housing.

Finally, those already involved with informal sector activity will be supported with training programmes. Their needs will also be taken into account during the partial relocation of families affected by the new road system as well as currently by flooding, so that they can continue with their activities. New Rest is, through its own efforts, one the informal settlements most visited by overseas tourists, and the community have agreements with a number of tour operators. Hence the development of services and the creation of goods for tourists is a further major development.

Technical Sustainability

Services have a cost attached to them and the provision of services as part of the upgrading process cannot be removed from the issue of affordability, and this in turn is linked to the issue of levels of service. The nature of the ground in this part of Cape Town means that some form of water-borne sewerage is the only option, making this service expensive. However, there are two ways of dealing with this wider issue that are being considered. The first is to reduce the road network significantly, and thereby reduce costs in this area. While there will be core network of roads, the majority will be small, one way roads or footpaths. The second is to take care in the appointment of the engineer. The normal discussion about services, often quoted in literature referring to the Orangi project in Karachi for example, juxtaposes the low cost of services in community driven projects with the high cost of services designed by external consultants. That is only partly true. There is also an issue of quality and it is questionable whether some of the examples quoted will necessarily be cheaper when costed on a total life cycle basis. The findings of this project are that the real issue with respect to costs is somewhat different. Here considerable savings have been made in the cost of services by working with committed consultants who work with the community on the ground. Thus they provide a site solution, rather than a generalised solution applied locally, and this is where the cost saving is made.

Exploring Organisational Alternatives

The body currently responsible for managing services in New Rest is the local authority. Because the financial and technical systems are centralised, and the same for all residents in the metropolitan area, this may not be suited to the needs of low-income communities. What is needed, and likely to be more appropriate, is a management system that is centred around the specific needs of individual communities. This is the model that is currently being developed in New Rest.

New Rest is demarcated by a single erf (site or parcel). Thus there is no need for consolidation of the land. At the same time, up-grading is a process of continuous change and does not lend itself to the up-front preparation of a surveyed site plan registred with the Surveyor General, which is necessary for individual subsidy applications (the norm in South Africa under the government's housing subsidy system). This can be overcome by using what is known as an institutional sub-sidy, where all the families apply collectively. However, it has raised the question in the community of future management of infrastructure, and led to a discussion within the community about how the needs of this specific community are to be addressed. As a result, the commu-nity is now exploring the possibility of managing the infrastructure themselves.

This has major benefits for the local authority. It means that the area can be supplied through a single water meter and a single account issued. The community body then becomes a bulk user and buys waster and electricity in bulk. It also relieves the local authority of direct responsibility for road maintenance, as well as maintenance of the stormwater system, sewer and road. For its part, the community can negotiate a single rates charge (a local tax on property) with the local authority, which would operate at a substantial discount to the individ-ual rates base. This approach is made possible because all the infor-mation pertaining to the infrastructure is already available and linked to the GIS system that has been established to manage the upgrading project. This goes down to the level of fittings and fixtures for the retic-ulation systems. Hence it is only a small step to creating an asset man-agement system and a maintenance programme. This is not far-fetched. The technology already exists within the project and the system is being structured in such a way as to make it possible.

Further Reading

Alder, G. (1995) "Tackling Poverty in Nairobi's Informal Settlements: developing an institutional strategy." *Environment and Urbanization* 7 (2), pp 85-107.

Abbott, J., Martinez, I. and Huchzermeyer, M. (2000) *The Application of Visual Settlement Planning in South Africa: Facilitating urban upgrading programmes and building the capacity of local communities.* Part 1: Analysis of informal settlements and the applicability of ViSP in South Africa, Cape Town, Pretoria: Water Research Commission (in press).

Abbott, J., Martinez, I. and Douglas, D. (2000) *The Application of Visual Settlement Planning in South Africa: Facilitating urban upgrading programmes and building the capacity of local communities.* Part 2: The upgrading methodology: a case study of New Rest, Cape Town, Pretoria: Water Research Commission (in press).

Freeman, Donald B. (1991) *A City of Farmers: Informal Urban Agriculture in the Open Spaces of Nairobi, Kenya.* Montreal: McGill-Queen's University Press.

Lee-Smith, D. (1990) "Squatter Landlords in Nairobi: A Case Study of Korogocho." In *Housing Africa's Urban Poor,* edited by P. Amis and P. Lloyd. Manchester and New York: Manchester University Press for the International African Institute.

CHAPTER 5

City planning and habitat

INTEGRATING LAND-USE PLANNING AND HOUSING

Land-use and housing have long been key elements of public intervention in urban management. They are also important components of town and country planning: zoning and land-use measures have often been used for urban management. Monitoring the impacts of planning and development control on urban processes and the built environment highlight challenging issues. This is particularly the case in municipalities which have attempted to protect themselves from new immigrant intakes, or those, like Toronto, that have tried integration policies.

When massive population flows occur in cities and when specific ethnic groups become excluded, then land-use and housing policies acquire a new dimension. They are a means to avoid chaotic urban development and the creation of ghettos. Policies are also integral components of the global urban context: the housing system is very much dependent on the other economic, social and institutional components of urban systems. In terms of urban prospects, long-term impacts can therefore be envisaged. Planning for housing implies evaluating the present system, predicting its evolution in relation to the interactions with other components of urban systems, and formulating strategies based on sustainable development. Such a global approach is increasingly part of planning strategies for 2010-2015 in cities including Geneva and Cape Town.

Housing policies also have to take into account factors such as quality and affordability, as described in studies from Geneva and

Rotterdam. New instruments to plan and finance housing developments ought to be applied, as in São Paulo.

It remains to be seen how these measures will avoid urban fragmentation in relation to the emergence of a two-tier society.

LAND USE STRATEGIES, HOUSING QUALITY AND AFFORDABILITY, PARTICIPATORY PROCESSES

In **Cape Town**, a co-ordinated approach to spatial planning has been formulated for the metropolitan area with a social perspective. Stewart Fisher identifies the potentials of the *Metropolitan Spatial Development Framework (MSDF)* to contribute to social, environmental and economic objectives, in addition to its primary thrust, which is spatial integration (see Chapter 5.1). This spatial strategy provides *"opportunities for economic and residential integration, as well as for social and cultural integration."* Its social goal is *"to integrate, socially and economically, the disparate communities of the metropolitan area and thereby engender greater social harmony."*

In **Geneva**, although strategic planning is dominated by economic and environmental concerns, nevertheless spatial plans include social objectives. Sophie Lin describes the social challenges which have been integrated in the preparation of the urban development Master Plan for the Geneva region (see Chapter 5.2). These social concerns include demographic development, functional and social mix, as well as factors of political and economic balance. Cross-border co-operation has been developed as a central component of the Master Plan. Based on a multi-nodal development model, collaboration with local authorities of the neighbouring areas of France is aimed at redressing employment and at improving urban quality of life in the whole region. This trans-national approach is a way to promote an integrated management of the city.

In the area of housing, a study in **Geneva** has focused on ways of better understanding and assessing the quality of urban housing. Roderick Lawrence notes that traditional approaches have concentrated either on *"the point of view of the individual, on material/quantifiable characteristics of housing, or on housing policy. Studies now need an integrated conceptual framework in which sets of architectural, demographic, economic, ecological and political factors are interrelated."* With this objective, the author examines *"what qualities of urban housing promote social sustainability"* and the wide range of elements encompassed in the complex notion of housing quality. The societal context of housing needs particular attention: *"It is necessary to replace urban and housing policies that have been largely based on the average or median by a more in-depth understanding of cultural, social and economic diversity in cities. This can be achieved by a contextual understanding based on the identification and then the aggregation of those factors that are implicated in the provision, affordability, management and tenure of housing in specific cities."*

In a household survey completed in Geneva in 1990 (see Chapter 5.3), the applied reference model is meant to achieve such an integrated interpretation of urban housing quality: *"This model includes the dimensions of the layout, design, tenure and effective use of housing in conjunction with those sets of contextual factors present. It integrates studies of architectural quality, residential satisfaction and user preference as well as diverse geographical scales and human dimensions of housing."*

The key findings of the survey are related *"to those means and measures that can be considered in terms of promoting more socially sustainable urban habitats."* They show *"why and how in-depth studies of the lifestyles, preferences and values of groups and individuals can be used to identify key issues that can become the main subjects of a research agenda to promote innovative means and measures in the Canton of Geneva."*

In **Rotterdam**, a study has focused on the Dutch social housing policy, *"which stands out in comparison with other countries in Western Europe."* Frans Dieleman analyses *"the relationship between the Dutch policy of mass production of social housing and some aspects of the social sustainability of cities."* After extensive support for social housing by both the national and local governments, recent housing policy changes have started to induce social impacts: *"an affordability problem for housing has risen under the new housing policy."*

The example of Rotterdam (see Chapter 5.4) illustrates the following four aspects of a sustainable housing provision:
   "(i) sufficient housing opportunities for households in low income brackets or out of employment;
   (ii) housing that is affordable in terms of the percentage of disposable income spent on shelter;

(iii) housing that, even if it is affordable, is of a reasonably good quality; and
(iv) housing where residential segregation by income and race is low.

The research highlights the successes and failures of the different housing policies with a focus on two topics:
"(i) the desirability and sustainability of an extremely large social housing stock; and
(ii) residential segregation."

Participatory systems have been applied to improve the housing situation in **São Paulo** and **Brasilia**. Nelson Saule examines the potential of such *"decentralised management systems with democratic and participatory management"* to develop and finance social housing development projects. The author also considers the potential of legislation accepted by popular initiative in the early 1990s for *"a national system of housing policy with the participation of representatives of housing movements (homeless, urban landless, favela residents), of the community and of non-governmental organisations."*

Two local initiatives are detailed (see Chapter 5.5) where a *"Housing Council was created, as an entity for direct community participation in housing management policy."* The dynamics induced by the creation of a Housing Council is *"to allow the community, which never before gathered at the same negotiating table, to get together."*

5.1   A Framework for Metropolitan Spatial Development in Cape Town

from Stewart Fisher, *"Integrated Development Planning in the Cape Metropolitan Area"*

Co-ordinated Responses to Planning and Development

In 1991, Cape metropolitan authorities, in conjunction with municipal and NGO role-players, identified the need to draft an overarching plan at the metropolitan level to guide the sub-metropolitan plans. This plan, termed the *Metropolitan Spatial Development Framework* (MSDF), was adopted by the Cape Metropolitan Council (CMC) in 1996 (see Figure 5.1).

Linkages with the Key Integrated Development Plan Themes

The *MSDF* targets the 5 key themes of the *Integrated Development Plan* (see Chapter 2.4). The Framework contributes to the following objectives:

Targeting Poverty and Homelessness

Through the development of activity corridors and nodes, the concept of the *MSDF* is that high density residential development will take place within walking distance of a range of economic activities and employment opportunities, as well as public transport. In regard to addressing homelessness, the *MSDF* has led to a study to determine vacant and strategic land, which could be made available for housing.

Strengthening the Cape Metropole's Global Economic Position

The *MSDF* is a metropolitan spatial development strategy adopted by the CMC. It is to provide clarity in respect of the form and location of future spatial growth in the metropolitan area over a 20-year development horizon. It provides an estimation of focused and committed public sector investment strategies, and hence confidence for both short- and long-term private investment strategies.

Enhancing the Environment

The spatial principles of urban management for sustainability and protecting the environment have their land-use implementation mechanisms in the *Urban Edge* and the *Metropolitan Open Space System* (MOSS) strategies. The *Urban Edge* strategy is, in part, intended to prevent urban sprawl into valuable environmental and agricultural

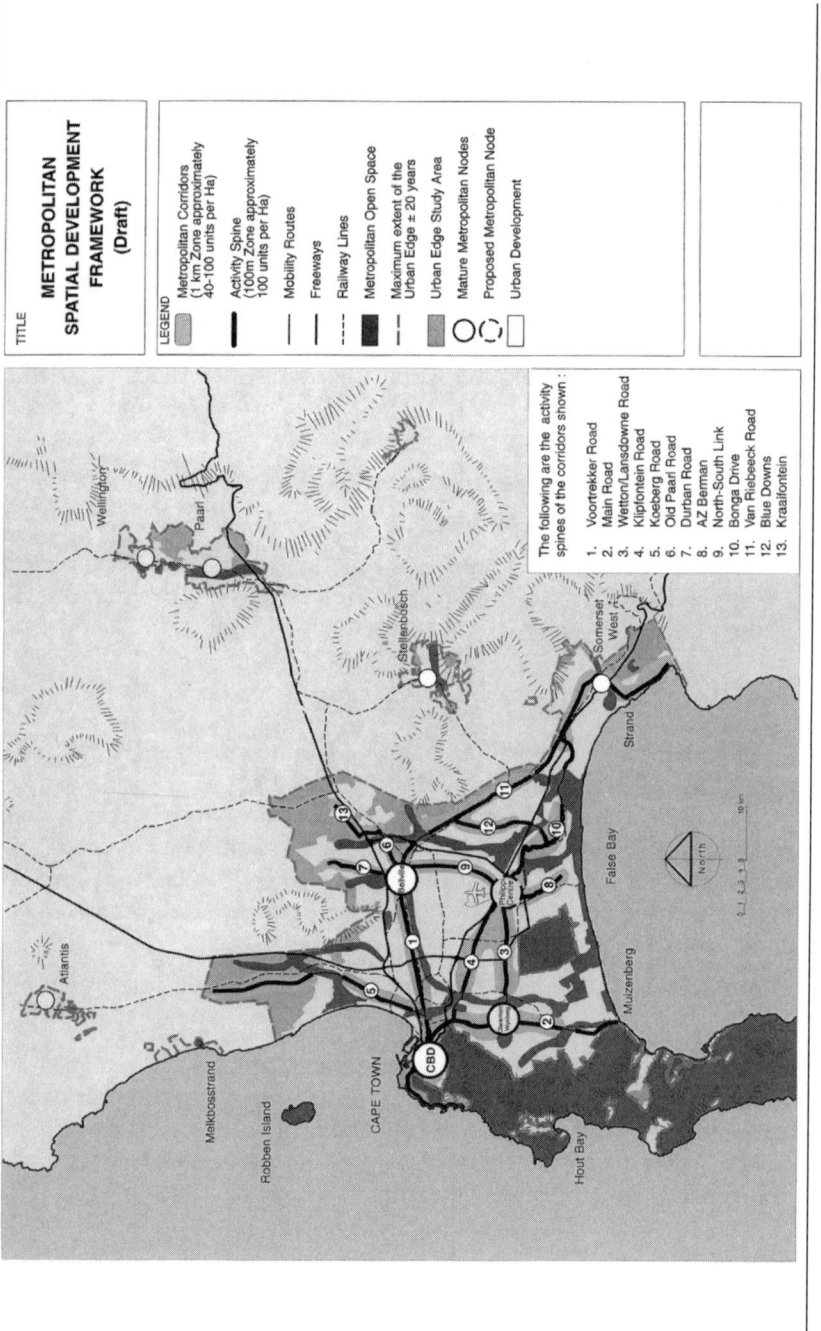

Source: Cape Metropolitan Council (1996)

Figure 5.1 **The Structuring Elements of the Cape**
"Metropolitan Spatial Development Framework"

resources. The *MOSS* is a strategy for providing recreation opportunities for residents of high-density suburbia, as well as a strategy to protect natural environments.

Building Social Harmony and Civic Responsibility

A primary goal of the *MSDF* is to socially and economically integrate the disparate communities of the metropolitan area, thereby engendering greater social cohesion. The spatial strategies for this are the linking corridors and integrating *MOSS* elements. The former provides opportunities primarily for economic and residential interaction and integration; the latter for social and cultural interaction and integration.

Developing Local Government

By involving key urban stakeholders in the participatory process and capacity building, the development of local government is enhanced. A significant *MSDF* implementation strategy has been that of educating and communicating the principles and concepts of the Framework. This has assisted in empowering officials with the knowledge and techniques to implement MSDF concepts and strategies.

Emerging Issues

The specific relationship between the *MSDF* and the key *IDP* themes reveals some interesting emerging issues. It is particularly important to note the strong interdependency of the *MSDF* with the housing process. The *MOSS* and the *Urban Edge* projects both depend on the success of the corridor/node implementation. Given the nature of the current rural-urban migration flow, failure to provide housing development at an adequate rate will lead to a rapid increase in land invasions, which will eventually encroach upon both the open space and the urban edge.

5.2   A Master Plan for Sustainable Development in Geneva

from Sophie Lin, *"The Master Plan of Geneva: Proposition for a Sustainable Development"*

Geneva's concept for urban development, part of the Cantonal Master Plan, is governed by the principles of sustainability. It is based on a three-fold strategy: giving co-ordinated and equal attention to social problems, environmental issues and economic matters.

In Geneva, the urban agenda is dominated by economic and environmental concerns, because social problems are not as acute as in some other cities. Social challenges are nevertheless present and have a bearing on the concept for urban development. These social concerns appear mainly in the three following policy areas:

First, in terms of *demographic development and related needs*: It is not possible to simply ignore demographic development in order to achieve environmental goals or to limit public expenditure. Population growth requires basic urban needs and these have to be met by planning.

Second, in terms of *functional and social mix*: The urban planning concept aims to bring local and international life closer together, a crucial objective for the multicultural Geneva. It involves planning for a mix of activities in the district of the international organisations or around international research centres such as the European Centre for Nuclear Research.

Policies have also been defined to promote the social and cultural integration of immigrant workers. In Geneva, the socially discriminating status of seasonal workers has been progressively abandoned, allowing the families of these workers to come and settle in the Canton. As a consequence, planning for new social housing programmes and schools is required.

Third, in terms of *political and economic balance*: Significant disparities exist at the communal level, between rich and poor urban authorities. This situation is made worse by a lack of co-operation between these communes. To address this issue, the Cantonal Master Plan puts forwards a global vision for future urban and regional development. However, a greater financial solidarity among the communes is required, in particular by improving the redistribution of tax revenue.

Another and even more important disparity exists between the Swiss and French communes on each side of the border — a richer area on the "Pays de Gex" side, and a poorer one on the "Haute Savoie" side. Policies have to redress the dependency of these areas

on the Swiss metropolitan centre which concentrates most employment.

   Cross-border co-operation is proposed in the Master Plan, based
on a multi-nodal development model (see Figure 5.2). The objective is
to encourage the development of quality nodes, well connected to the
public transport network. This high-quality public service is a way to
attract businesses and create employment. The expected outcome is to
redress the employment balance and to improve quality of life in the
suburban areas.

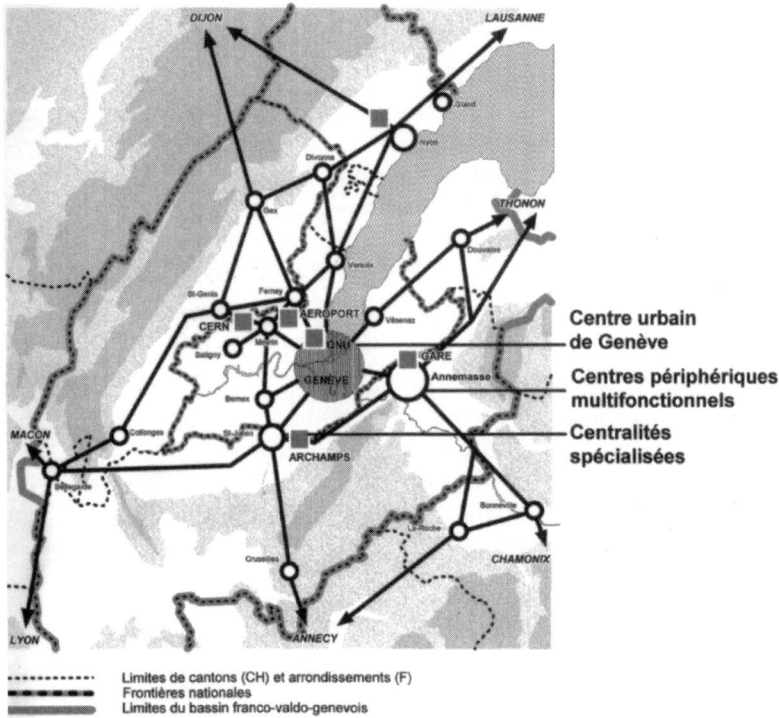

Figure 5.2 **Multi-nodal Development for the Geneva Cross-border Area:**
multi-functional and specialised centres on the outskirts of Geneva

5.3   Towards a Comprehensive Understanding of Urban Housing Quality in Geneva

from Roderick J. Lawrence, *"Qualities of Urban Habitats and Socially Sustainable Development: Key Issues from a Survey in the Canton of Geneva"*

Geneva and the Swiss Housing Context

A recent comparative study of new housing construction found that costs were 29% higher in Switzerland than in Germany for comparable flats. Those higher costs were attributed to local customs in the construction sector, building construction standards and regulations, different bathroom and kitchen equipment, and higher professional fees.

The predominant form of housing tenure in Switzerland has been, and still is, rental tenure in the private sector (68.7% rented housing compared to 31.3% of owner-occupied housing units in 1990). Co-operative tenure has been relatively insignificant and invariant (3.9% in 1990). These national averages do not indicate disparities between urban and rural regions, nor between large cities and small towns. The share of owner-occupied housing in the Canton of Geneva was merely 13.8% in 1990.

In 1990, at least two-thirds of the rental housing stock was owned by private individuals. However, there has been a steady decline in this type of ownership. Limited property companies, associations and institutions have assumed an increasing role in the rental housing sector, whereas ownership by the Swiss Confederation, Cantons, and Communes declined (by 2.7% in 1990). In Geneva, in 1990, public authorities did not own more than 4.9% of the housing stock.

During the 20th century the size of rental housing units increased, whereas the numbers of persons per household declined (see Figure 5.3). Three-roomed housing units have consistently been the predominant size in recent decades (27.4% in 1990). The proportion of housing units with four rooms increased (26.8% in 1990), whereas the share of housing units with one and two rooms has remained virtually constant at about 20%. These trends can be contrasted with the steady decline in household size and, especially, the growing share of households with one and two persons. In 1990, the average square metres of habitable floor space per person was 40 square metres for the Canton of Geneva.

As for the composition and size of households in the Canton of Geneva in 1990, 67.5% of all households comprised one or two persons, and 44% of the resident population lived in these households. Census returns for 1990 indicate an average of 2.2 persons per household.

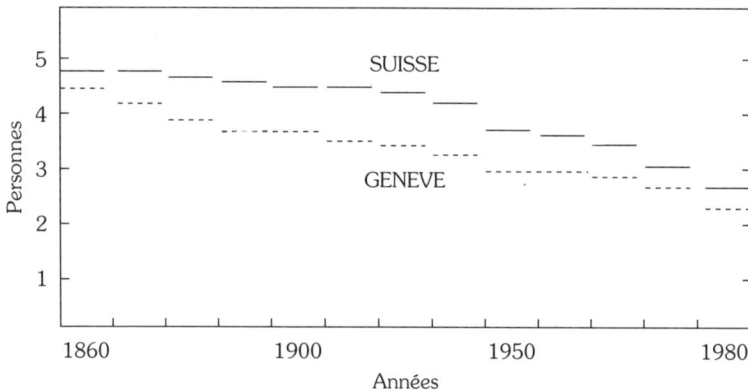

Figure 5.3 **Household Size in Geneva:** steady decline of the number of persons
per household since 1860, in Switzerland and in the Canton of Geneva
in particular (by kind permission of the Cantonal Office of Statistics)

Household Survey in the Canton of Geneva

A survey of 525 households residing in the Canton of Geneva was
completed in 1990 in order to ascertain how and why a representative
sample of the population defined, ordered and evaluated the components of their daily surroundings. The survey was limited to rental
housing in both the public and private sectors, and it was conducted in
the domicile of the respondents. A questionnaire with directed, semi-
directed and open-ended questions was used. It included seven main
parts (interviewer checklist; household demography; past residential
experience; current professional and leisure activities; rooms fittings
and uses; residential building and facilities; neighbourhood, in particular public and private services and nuisances)

The findings of the survey have been used to formulate a new
research agenda based on the following key issues:

- Is residential mobility pertinent for socially sustainable
  development in a precise locality?

More than 80% of the respondents were satisfied or very satisfied with their housing unit, the residential building and their neighbourhood. However, 42.9% expressed the wish to move. As residential mobility can have significant economic and social impacts
for public authorities, property owners and tenants, this factor is relevant to socially sustainable development in specific localities.

The wish to move can be (at least partly) understood if the age, length
of tenure, past residential experience, housing availability and affordability, as well as effective occupancy conditions are considered. The 1990

survey found that the location of the housing unit, its cost, and personal relations with neighbours were apparently not significant in determining whether the respondents wished to move. Although fiscal reasons may play a role, other equally important factors used by specific groups of the population (e.g. the elderly) need to be studied in order to explain why they are satisfied but would still like to move elsewhere in the same neighbourhood, or within, or outside the Canton of Geneva.

- *Are housing tenure and management customs relevant for socially sustainable development?*

The 1990 survey found that not less than 35% of respondents had access to two residences. Although the majority of them spent more time in their urban residence, it was not attributed the same affective meaning as the residence used less frequently in the countryside. Those who have access to two residences are generally less critical of both the design and management components of their urban housing unit, of its immediate surroundings and the services and facilities.

This finding illustrates the important role of trade-offs between utilitarian, economic and symbolic dimensions of everyday life. It also suggests that if a secondary/holiday residence is used as a place to satisfy unmet needs in urban habitats, then there can be significant socio-psychological consequences for the resident population, as well as unintended economic and environmental impacts on ecosystems outside the Canton of Geneva. Socially sustainable development will not be achieved unless these unmet needs are recognised by policy-makers.

- *Can renovation and personalisation promote more socially sustainable development?*

Only 2.9% of all respondents were very unsatisfied with their housing unit, the residential building and the urban neighbourhood. This can be explained to a large extent by the age of the residential building, the layout-type of the flat, effective occupancy conditions and the social status of the neighbourhood. The survey in 1990 did not find a direct relationship between housing quality and the rent. There was no distinction between the appreciation of housing units that had or had not been renovated.

These findings show that the respondents have the capacity to critically scrutinise and evaluate (negatively) specific aspects of their everyday surroundings while expressing an overall (positive) assessment. Irrespective of the financial cost of up-grading the housing stock, there is an urgent need to reconsider current renovation projects and upgrading practices which have not taken into account the point-of-view of the resident population.

- *Can personal initiative overcome the commodification of rental housing?*

The 1990 survey was meant to identify and account for decisions prior to and during the planning of housing units and residential buildings; the history of housing from initial occupation, including modifications to structure, decoration, fittings; the residents' past experience, stages in the life-cycle and goals.

No relationship was found between the age of the residential building and whether the respondents had made changes. The numbers and kinds of changes are not related to the age, gender, or socio-professional status of the respondents, whereas the number of changes increased as the length of the tenancy increased. The largest share of all changes occurred in the living room, irrespective of its size, shape or relative position in the flat.

As many tenants are willing to invest their time and resources in order to personalise their housing unit and modify it during the course of their life-cycle, it would be instructive to study those means and measures that could enable the redefinition of the roles and responsibilities of tenants in private rental housing. This would reduce the cost of housing, and therefore be a step towards more socially sustainable development.

This type of in-depth study of the lifestyles, preferences and values of groups and individuals can be used to identify key issues that can become the main subjects of a research agenda to promote innovative means and measures in the Canton of Geneva. Such an integrated approach (see Figure 5.4) can enable professionals, politicians and citizens to develop a more comprehensive understanding of the qualitative aspects of urban habitats.

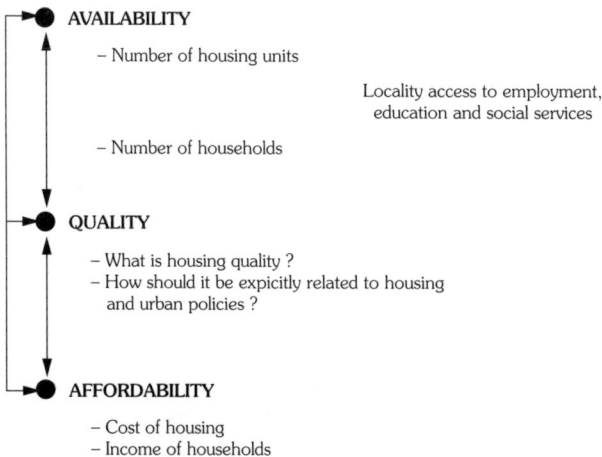

AVAILABILITY

– Number of housing units

Locality access to employment, education and social services

– Number of households

QUALITY

– What is housing quality ?
– How should it be expicitly related to housing and urban policies ?

AFFORDABILITY

– Cost of housing
– Income of households

Figure 5.4 **An Integrated Approach to Housing Quality:** *recognising the interrelated nature of housing affordability, availability and the quantitative aspects of residential environments*

5.4   Impacts of Policies for Social Housing in Rotterdam

from Frans M. Dieleman, *"Can Housing Policy Help to Create Socially Sustainable Cities? Experiences from Rotterdam"*

Social Housing in the Netherlands

After 1950, rapid population growth and rising affluence led to a large expansion of the Dutch housing stock. Diverse coalition governments emphasised the mass production of social housing at a pace unequalled elsewhere in Europe. The social rented sector now accounts for 41% of the Dutch housing stock, and over 50% in cities like Amsterdam and Rotterdam. While 45% of the total stock is owner-occupied, the private rental sector has declined to 13%.

This policy of mass production can only be understood in relation to a wider policy of economic growth and social accommodation which the government pursued from the 1960s through to the 1980s. Housing was used as an instrument of anti-cyclical policies in periods of economic downturn and as means to reach a compromise on broader economic and social issues.

This policy was made instrumental in three main ways: large national subsidies for the new construction and operation of social housing units; the system of rent control (on average 10-12% of the disposable income is for rent); the creation of housing associations. These instruments were supplemented by a system of housing allowances and an extensive system of subsidies for the renewal of the older parts of the urban housing stock (see Figure 5.5).

The political support for extensive government intervention in the housing market and for large housing subsidies eroded over the 1980s, as shown in the aims of the 1989 Housing Memorandum:
  • *Retreat of the public sector:* by making the housing associations more independent and by devolving the authority for housing provision to the municipal governments.
  • *Reliance on market forces*: by increasing rent above the level of inflation; by reducing the financial ties between the national government and the housing associations; and by tapering off or abolishing subsidies for new construction.
  • *Selective use of subsidies*: by targeting support on the households at the bottom of the income scale, and by proposing an incentive to stimulate middle- and higher-income households to leave the low-cost part of the social rented housing stock.
  • *Promotion of home ownership.*

These changes do not mean that all national government involvement in the housing market has come to an end. The rent subsidy to individual households is still in place. Rent increases in large parts of the rental sector remain under government control.

Photos: Frank van Wensveen (1999)

Figure 5.5 **Pre-war Social Housing and 1960s High-rise Social Housing**

Four Aspects of Socially Sustainable Housing in Rotterdam

Good Housing Opportunities for Low Incomes

In Rotterdam, the policy of mass production of social housing has created a situation where there are ample housing opportunities for the low-income groups. Even with the recent rent increases induced by changes in national housing policy, affordable housing is still abundant. Groups like immigrants (now 24% of the population of the city of Rotterdam), who have suffered from high unemployment rates, largely live in the social rented sector. However, the production of new rental housing units with a reasonable price has also dwindled in Rotterdam as a result of the reduction in housing subsidies at the national level. In 1998 the construction of more expensive dwellings predominates.

Affordability of Housing

Rotterdam has a relatively low-cost (rental) housing stock. However, even in this situation households could not escape the effects of the rent increases induced by national housing policy from 1980. On average, Rotterdam family households receiving housing allowances in 1994 still paid 20% of their disposable income for rent (22% for single-parent families; 28% for persons living alone; 40-50% for specific groups). Rather than demonstrating that a housing allowance helps to redress housing affordability problems for many, the large number of recipients (29% of all households) indicates that the massive social housing stock of the city no longer provides affordable housing for everyone.

Housing Quality

Under the urban renewal grant scheme of the national government, the city of Rotterdam embarked on a programme of buying the older stock from the private owners, in order to renovate it and make it part of the social rented sector. The recent changes in national housing policy have put this programme under pressure. It is expected that not all of the funds for the necessary future repairs will be available. However, in general, and taking the Rotterdam situation as a reference, one can conclude that the extensive subsidisation of housing in the Netherlands has certainly helped to keep the housing stock in good condition and that many households with relatively modest resources profit from it.

Residential Segregation

It has sometimes been argued that the Dutch policy of mass production of social housing has been instrumental in avoiding the extreme forms of residential segregation emerging elsewhere. In cities like Rotterdam and Amsterdam the sector is so large that it also houses many median and even higher incomes. However, if one looks at the geographical concentration of the immigrant population in Rotterdam at the mid-1990s, this viewpoint is debatable. If one takes all the ethnic minorities as one group, the concentration of the immigrant population in some census tracts is quite high. The segregation index (43 at the neighbourhood level) is comparable to that in other West European cities. Therefore, the large social rented housing stock in Rotterdam certainly seems to help in the provision of reasonably decent housing for the immigrant population, but this state-led protection against market forces has not, however, safeguarded them from spatial segregation.

Evaluating Success and Failures of the Dutch Housing Policies

Mass Production of Social Housing

The main advantage of the Dutch policy is that social housing was not stigmatised as shelter for the underprivileged. A large stable group of tenants, amply able to pay the rents, created an enviable situation for housing associations, as a social landlord held in high esteem by both the tenants and the politicians.

The democratic control and public accountability of housing associations are among less positive aspects: Who can control these often very large legally private organisations? To whom are they accountable for their actions and corporate strategies? How does one measure the performance of individual housing associations and their management? The discipline exerted by the market forces on the practises of businesses penetrates the social housing sector. Some authors now even voice their concern that housing associations might become too oriented towards pursuing a financially sound course, and ignore their social objectives too much.

With the increasing attractiveness of home-ownership, the clientele of housing associations is eroding. The dwindling role of social housing is a matter of concern, especially for associations in cities: they might find it hard to adjust to these changes, because the social housing stock is so large and many dwellings are in high-rise estates which are difficult to rent on the market.

Social Housing and Residential Segregation

Social housing in Dutch cities is not a sector in which only the poor live. However, within the sector itself, segregation by income occurs.

The process of the increasing concentration of low-income house-holds, and a generally diminishing presence of middle- and high-incomes, can also be demonstrated in the Dutch social rented sector. The recent changes in housing policy can be expected to accelerate this process of change of occupancy in this sector.

In the case of Rotterdam, the question: *"can a model of mass pro-duction of social housing help to create socially sustainable cities?"* has an ambiguous answer. Undoubtedly, many households in various income brackets have lived in this sector to their satisfaction. More recently, those out of work and with low incomes could find decent shelter in the large social housing stock. However there are doubts about the viability of such a large social housing sector in the future, now that housing policy has changed, and rents have been raised to near market level. Many middle-income households are now leaving this sector. The predicted growing affluence of the Dutch population may make part of the sector redundant in the 21st century.

5.5 Participatory Housing Management in Brasilia and São Paulo

from Nelson Saule Jr., *"Democratic and Participative System of Housing Management Policy — Brazilian Experiences"*

Participatory Housing Management in Brasilia

Inadequate Housing Infrastructure Provision

Housing problems in Brasilia increased between 1989 and 1994, when the Federal Government promoted an uncontrolled programme of the distribution of public lands, creating various settlements, many of them without any infrastructure. These irregular human settlements presented the following problems: irregular land and property ownership; absence of water supply; lack of domestic and storm sewerage; lack of electricity services and refuse collection; inadequate street infrastructure; and occupation of areas designated for environmental preservation.

With the construction of these settlements the number of urban housing units with inadequate infrastructure has reached 100,000. Furthermore, some 6,000 families reside in irregular housing units in areas of risk, with precarious construction conditions, difficult access, sanitation problems and without community facilities.

This situation was aggravated by the fact that 100,000 low-income families received lots in settlements and have no document to guarantee ownership. This situation impedes access to financing for the improvement and construction of housing, and causes insecurity. It is also harmful to family life and discourages household investment in housing.

Participatory Tools: The Housing Council and Housing Fund

A democratic process was established to confront the housing problem. A *District Housing Conference* took place in 1996, involving the participation of some 10,000 persons active in the housing sector. A *Housing Council* and a *Federal Housing Fund* were established as fundamental instruments in the housing policy management system.

The *Housing Council*, composed of representatives of various groups and institutions, is a democratic management tool that seeks to guarantee equal participation of society in the preparation and implementation of housing policy.

The *Council* has a predominantly political nature, because it allows the co-ordinated and integrated action among the various agencies of the Federal District Government for the development of housing policy. It has power to make decisions concerning: housing guidelines, strategies and policy priorities; allocation of resources; evaluation of the economic and financial management of approved programmes and projects; the set of projects and proposals for intervention; resources for social housing projects; financing and subsidisation policy, etc.

The *Housing Fund* is an essential instrument of the housing policy management system that seeks to guarantee resources to finance the social housing programmes and projects of the Federal District. Its purpose is also to provide basic urban infrastructure and community equipment linked to the housing projects.

Resources should be allocated for: urbanisation, building and land regularisation of low-income housing settlements; production of urbanised lots with infrastructure; physical improvement; community facilities; purchase of construction materials; acquisition of land; emergency housing services; technical and legal assistance services to non-profit community organisations; partnerships with community associations and co-operatives, non-governmental organisations and unions.

The *Housing Conference* sought to assure a broad and democratic process of social participation in the preparation and evaluation of public policy. The goal was to mobilise the government and civil society to discuss, evaluate and formulate guidelines and mechanisms of democratic housing policy, and establish this tool as a component of housing policy management. The Conference will be held every two years in order to evaluate and define actions.

Participatory Housing Management in Diadema, São Paulo

Rapid and Unorganised Urban Growth

The Municipality of Diadema is part of the São Paulo Metropolitan Region. Twenty-six percent of its territory is composed of wetlands, defined by state laws as areas of environmental preservation. With a large concentration of automobile and manufacturing firms, the city attracted an important flow of migrant workers. Between 1960 and 1990, the area of Diadema grew at a rate of almost 16% per year in an unorganised fashion through the establishment of illegal sub-divisions and favelas which lack urban infrastructure. There are 192 favelas in the municipality, in which some 95,000 residents live.

These areas of precarious housing lack infrastructure or basic sanitation; they face problems of lighting and have difficult access to residences. The strong demand for housing has provoked the multiplication of clandestine subdivisions and the appropriation of public and private land by the needy population.

In recent years, violent conflicts have increased in relation to these housing problems. They have involved private landowners, the government — due to the occupation of public areas and those protected as wetlands — and the population.

The formation of various popular housing, homeless and favela movements in all regions of the city has constituted an expressive political force in the municipality (see Figure 5.6). Nevertheless, the absence of sufficient financial resources in the municipality has generated a permanent process of conflict and negotiation between the population and the local government.

Photo: Evaniza Rodrigues - National Housing Movement Union

Figure 5.6 **Mobilisation of the Housing Movement Union in São Paulo City to Defend the Implementation of Low-income Housing Programmes**

Participatory Tools:
Community Projects and the Housing Council

The construction of popular housing has been defined by the Municipal Government of Diadema as an important goal. It has defined as a priority the implementation of favela urbanisation programmes and the democratisation of access to urban land.

Community work projects have been encouraged. A construction materials co-operative has been created. Assistance was offered to the

Homeless Movement for the acquisition of areas of social interest. Organising the population into associations, with a management democratically elected by the residents, has been a precondition for involvement by the municipal government in projects.

Participatory Tools:
Community Projects and the Housing Council

The construction of popular housing has been defined by the Municipal Government of Diadema as an important goal. It has defined as a priority the implementation of favela urbanisation programmes and the democratisation of access to urban land.

Community work projects have been encouraged. A construction materials co-operative has been created. Assistance was offered to the Homeless Movement for the acquisition of areas of social interest. Organising the population into associations, with a management democratically elected by the residents, has been a precondition for involvement by the municipal government in projects.

A *Housing Council* has been established. It is composed of four representatives of the municipal administration and five representatives of housing movements in Diadema, who are elected by the regional associations. A representative of the City Council is elected for a two-year mandate.

The Council is responsible for approving guidelines for managing a Housing Fund, making decisions about its resources and the monitoring of investments. The Council is a forum for debating issues proposed by the housing movement representatives and new issues and proposals about housing policy.

The Council's achievements can be summarised as follows:
- urbanisation projects in 120 of the 192 existing favelas in the city, benefiting 19,991 families of the 23,342 living there;
- the acquisition of social interest areas or the appropriation of areas, in order to serve families removed from areas of risk;
- the acquisition of the "right to use for housing purposes" in lands of 78 urbanised favelas by 5,838 families, through titles for concession to the right to use;
- some 80% of the projects were implemented with some form of direct participation by the population, or through their associations.

The following general points of criticism can be made about the process of democratisation of housing management policy:
- the difficulty of offering broad *access to information* about the projects, in particular to the local representatives;

- the difficulty of establishing a *systematic working dynamic* in the Council, due to the numerous conflict situations demanding an immediate response;
- the difficulty that the representatives of the popular movements have in *reconciling the institutional demands generated by the participatory process* in the Council, with their traditional local community work.

Further Reading

Cape Metropolitan Council (1996) *Metropolitan Spatial Development Framework: A Guide for Spatial Development in the Cape Metropolitan Functional Region.* Cape Town: CMC.

Canton Geneva (1996), *Projet 2015: Concept de l'aménagement cantonal.* Consultation Paper, Geneva: DAEL-Canton de Genève.

Danermark, B. and Elander, I. (eds) (1994) *Social Rented Housing in Europe: Policy, Tenure and Design.* Delft: Delft University Press.

Dieleman, F.M. (1994) *"Social Rented Housing: Valuable Asset or Unsustainable Burden?" Urban Studies* 31 (3), 447-464.

Dieleman, F.M. and Kloosterman, R.C. (2000) *"Room to Manoeuvre; Governance, Post-industrial Economy, Housing Provision in Rotterdam."* In *The Social Sustainability of Cities: Diversity and the Mangement of Change,* edited by M. Polèse and R. Stren. Toronto: University of Toronto Press.

Dieleman F.M. (1996) *"The Quiet Revolution in Dutch Housing Policy." Journal of Economic and Social Geography* 87, 275-282.

Fernandes, E. (1995) *Illegal Cities: Law and Urban Change in Brazil.* Aldershot: Avebury.

Lawrence, R. (1986) *Le Seuil franchi... : logement populaire et vie quotidienne en Suisse romande, 1860-1960.* Geneva: Georg Editeur.

Lawrence, R. (1987) *Housing, Dwellings and Homes: Design Theory, Research and Practice.* Chichester: John Wiley.

Priemus, H. (1995) *"How to Abolish Social Housing? The Dutch Case."* International Journal of Urban and Regional Research 19 (1), 145-155.

Santos, B. S. (1992) *"Law, State and Urban Struggles in Recife, Brazil."* Social & Legal Studies 1.

Saule Jr., N. (1997) *Novas Perspectivas do Direito Urbanístico Brasileiro. Ordenamento Constitucional da Política Urbana, Aplicação e Eficácia do Plano Diretor.* Porto Alegre: Sergio Antonio Fabris.

Saule Jr., N. (1999) *Direito à Cidade — Trilhas Legais para o direito ás cidades sustentáveis.* São Paulo: Max Limnonad/Instituto Pólis.

CHAPTER 6

Urban transport
and accessibility

FRAGMENTED CITY *VS.* INTEGRATED CITY

The functionalist vision of urban transport, essentially based on the "structuring effect" concept, has gradually been replaced by a social vision of urban transport. To what extent does transport, in particular public transport, ensure better accessibility for all citizens in the context of global urban trends? Accessibility from the most deprived areas to the city centre as in Nairobi, or accessibility to employment districts as in Cape Town, are important objectives of urban integration.

Any infrastructure provision can be considered simultaneously within the scope of long-term structural trends and within the strategies of stakeholders who adjust to, or influence, these developments. The notion of congruence is central to a socially sustainable vision of urban development, because the structuring impacts of large-scale infrastructures happen in, and modify, an economic and social system. The movement of people, information and goods, as well as interactions at the local level, are transformed, acting on the development of some areas and delaying it in others. In every city with large infrastructure networks, these interactions can become major issues: for example, in Lyon with the motorway by-pass built through social housing areas, or in Geneva with its motorway ring road.

Different transport systems are managed by multiple stakeholders, who favour their vested interests. Some aim for profitability, others favour social objectives to improve the socio-spatial accessibility of the city. Metropolitan areas today have to deal with problems related to the use of infrastructure, as well as the drawbacks and benefits to the user. These issues are to be addressed over the short-, middle- and long-term, as well as at various geographical levels (neighbourhood, city, metropole). Budapest's experience shows the importance of metropolitan co-ordination for transport infrastructure development.

The management of socially sustainable urban transport needs to focus on efficient mobility, on accessibility to the whole urban area, and also to pay attention to the impacts of infrastructure on the quality of urban life. In order to build an integrated city, municipal authorities ought to consider traffic and land-use policies simultaneously.

SOCIAL IMPACTS OF URBAN TRANSPORT POLICIES

In **Nairobi**, the lack of an affordable public transport system has for many years had significant social impacts; in particular it has played an important part in social exclusion. Diana Lee-Smith and Davinder Lamba examine this aspect of social transformation and describes *"the mechanics of social and spatial exclusion in relation to transport"* (see Chapter 6.1).

The authors show the deficiencies of public transport policy: *"neither the bus service nor the planning of mobility and traffic in the city was geared towards the needs of the majority African population."* A response has come from the private sector with the development of a local pirate taxi service. This form of transport has, however, never been fully incorporated into city planning and has suffered from bribery.

The social impacts of urban transport are at the centre of **Cape Town**'s integrated planning process. Stewart Fisher highlights the key role of transport policy as a mechanism for reducing poverty, one of the main objectives of the proposed Cape Metropolitan Transport Plan, "Moving Ahead" (see Chapter 6.2). It aims *"to redress the unequal distribution of, and access to, employment (and other urban) opportunities by directing public and private investment into areas of greatest need. Key strategic intervention focus areas are corridors and nodes in which mixed land-use coupled with residential intensification are encouraged."*

"Moving Ahead" will contribute to reducing poverty by improving and developing the public transport network. However, Fisher notes that *"in terms of effective implementation it is essential that the land-use, economic development and transport planning frameworks, as well as the housing delivery process are integrated."*

In **Budapest**, a motorway network has been very difficult to complete because of governance problems between the local authorities of the metropolitan area. György Enyedi shows that *"the usual environmental or economic concerns are exaggerated by the suburban municipalities"* antagonism towards the dominating capital city.*"*

This Budapest case study (see Chapter 6.3) is an example of the importance of the negotiation process for the achievement of a large transport infrastructure project. *"The story of this magisterial highway network illustrates the necessity of co-operation and communication in regional-type planning. It was a valuable — and so far unique — experience for all the participants in the discussion: how to reach consensus among partners with conflicting interests."*

In **Geneva**, a study has focused on the spatial and social impacts of transport. Antoine Bailly questions the functionalist vision that prevailed in the past: *"for a long time, transport has been considered as essential for town planning on the assumption that the creation of transport infrastructures automatically generates effects on the city and on the quality of life."* In reality, *"large transport infrastructure is a necessary condition for development, but not a sufficient condition."* The analysis of impacts shows that *"it is illusory to separate the effects of large transport infrastructures from those of the evolution of the urban environment"* because transport infrastructures are *"at the same time the result and the product of an existing social system."*

Geneva's case study (see Chapter 6.4) illustrates that *"the constitutive elements of the analysis should be diverse, in order to take into account the transformations of urban space."*

6.1   Impacts of Poor Transport Infrastructure Planning and Maintenance in Nairobi

from Diana Lee-Smith and Davinder Lamba, *"Social Transformation in a Post-Colonial City: The Case of Nairobi"*

A Deficient Public Transport Monopoly

In the colonial city, there were plans for buses as early as 1932, but public support was insufficient and costs too high. In 1934, the Kenya Bus Service (KBS) began operation as a private concern, part of a British multinational. Its arrangements with the Municipal Council included its legal monopoly over public transport and a 25% city stake in the company.

The service expanded steadily from its original two buses in 1934 to 140 in 1968. However, neither the bus service nor the planning of mobility and traffic in the city in general was always geared towards the needs of the majority African population. Most workers were unable to afford bus fares and consequently walked to work because they could not afford bicycles. However, there was no provision for footpaths in the planning or building of roads in Nairobi, in total disregard for people's needs and safety. Roads were planned for the use of motor vehicles used by the settlers, with drains at the side and seldom any space for walking.

A Flexible and Affordable Private Taxi Service

In 1973, a presidential decree recognised *matatus*, local pirate taxis. It was a response to their popularity, both in meeting people's needs for a more flexible and adaptive form of public transport and as a form of (self-)employment for the urban work force. For the first decade of independence before the decree, they had operated illegally. After another decade, the 1984 Traffic (Amendment) Act increased the recognition of the *matatus* but they have never been fully incorporated into city planning and continue to suffer harassment by police. In 1982 they paid three times as much in bribes to policemen as the public revenue they generated.

The Matatu Vehicle Owners Association became a powerful force in civil society, and the government attempted to suppress it at various times after the change of leadership at the national level in 1978. The size of vehicle fleets expanded in the 1980s and the predominantly Kikuyu owners and operators became more powerful political players as the movement for political reform mounted in the 1990s.

Sharing the Transport Market

In 1982, KBS buses were used for 27% of all trips, *matatus* for 23%, private cars for 22%, and bicycles or scooters for 4%, while 24% of the trips were on foot because of the high cost of transport. In 1991, although the bus company fleet had expanded to 300 vehicles, its market share had declined. Its competitors were the Nyayo Bus Corporation, a parastatal, and the *matatus*. While the *matatus* had overtaken the KBS with 57% market share in public transport compared to 40%, the Nyayo Bus Corporation only had 3% and later collapsed.

Protests over Poor Infrastructure and Police Harassment

As a result of the political conflicts over control of City Hall in the 1990s, public infrastructure, including roads, has been poorly maintained, with some roads in the city becoming impassable. *Matatu* operators have raised fares and staged strikes in protest, with passengers refusing to pay the high fares. *Matatu* operators have also staged protests over police harassment and extortion by youth wingers from the ruling political party, KANU.

Owing to police corruption and increasing lawlessness in the city, as well as a lack of planning and road maintenance, the general public suffers with long and hazardous journeys to work. Those who walk many kilometres every day still lack access footpaths, not to mention bicycle paths, demonstrating that Nairobi City Council has not emerged from the heritage of colonial planning.

6.2   An Integrated Transport System for the Cape Metropolitan Area

from Stewart Fisher, *"Integrated Development Planning in the Cape Metropolitan Area"*

The Moving Ahead Project

To fully integrate the various elements of transport in a holistic way, and also to involve role-players to a greater extent than was previously the case, the *Moving Ahead* process was initiated in 1995 as a statutory requirement of emerging national and provincial legislation. The report, at this stage almost completely drafted, will constitute an integrated transport plan for the Cape Metropole based on the *Metropolitan Spatial Development Framework* (see Chapter 5.1 for details on this project).

Linkages with the Integrated Development Plan Themes

Moving Ahead targets the five key themes of the *Integrated Development Plan* (see Chapter 2.4 for details). The project contributes to the following objectives:

Targeting Poverty and Homelessness

The primary way in which *Moving Ahead* targets poverty is by establishing a basic network of affordable public transport services through subsidies.

The plan targets homelessness by promoting the provision of accessible low-income housing along public transport corridors, particularly adjacent to interchanges (see Figure 6.1).

Moving Ahead also targets: a reduction in travel distances over time; a minimum percentage of disposable income required for daily transport needs; employment creation in local communities; economic growth within public transport corridors and around interchanges.

Strengthening the Cape Metropole's Global Economic Position

The global economic position of the Cape Metropolitan Area will be strengthened by providing adequate and well-maintained metropolitan transport networks and links to the economic hinterland. The port and airport in particular have the potential to further develop into Southern African freight and passenger hubs.

Photo: Cape Metropolitan Council

Figure 6.1 **Commuters at Cape Town Minibus Taxi Terminus**

A world-class, effective and efficient transport system connecting major tourist destinations is to be developed. The productivity of the work force will also be enhanced through an efficient, effective, safe and affordable public transport system.

Enhancing the Environment

Moving Ahead will enhance the environment through ensuring that the public transport system is an attractive, safe and viable alternative to commuting by car. The shift towards public transport will reduce pollution emissions and limit urban sprawl by encouraging people to live in proximity to the public transport-oriented corridors. It will also reduce delays on the road network.

Building Social Harmony and Civic Responsibility

The long-term transport plan ought to: meet the needs of current and future users; be considered socially acceptable and affordable; include a quality charter; offers security; be operated in the public interest and recognise the special needs of the poor, the elderly and the disabled.

Other potential targets are a reduction in accident rates, crowding and crime on public transport, and an increased compliance with all traffic regulations.

Developing Local Government

A new Land Transport Bill devolves many powers and functions to Provincial Governments. To fulfil the requirements of the Bill, a Metropolitan Transport Authority (MTA) will be established to undertake a much wider range of planning, operational, monitoring, marketing and funding functions than is currently the case.

With adequate resources, the MTA will have the potential to plan and implement an integrated transport system for the Cape Metropolitan Area.

Emerging Issues

The goals of the *Moving Ahead* project can only be achieved if there is a large injection of capital into the transport system. This can only come from two sources: national government or increased local revenue. Hence there is a strong primary dependency on increased economic activity and also on the dual elements, spatial and transport, of corridor development.

6.3   Metropolitan Compromise
to Complete the M0 Motorway around Budapest

from György Enyedi, *"Budapest Metropolitan Region"*

An Incomplete Ring Motorway

The idea to build a ring motorway around the capital city was first formulated in the 1970s. The main purpose was to detour the through traffic from the city centre.

The idea had great relevance for Budapest, because:
• all the Hungarian motorways started from Budapest;
• all the motorways have had significant international traffic, connecting Western and Central Europe to Eastern Europe and the Balkans;
• all the through traffic had to cross the city centre because there was no bridge to the south of Budapest within 100 kilometres.

There was general consensus that the construction should start in the south. The construction of the northern half seemed to be less urgent and the project was not well elaborated. Construction started in 1986. The first portion was opened in 1990, the second one in 1994. Two new bridges were built across the Danube: the M1 (western) and the M5 (Balkans) motorways became interconnected. However, the continuation of the motorway to the east has been blocked by conflicting interests.

A Series of Rejected Proposals

East Project 1

City Hall suggested building the motorway within the city because of the shorter length, lower construction costs, the possibility to use it also for intra-urban traffic, and saving the road construction costs in the local budget. The plan provoked harsh resistance from the residents of the outer districts: the motorway would be too close to the residential areas and they were also afraid of declining residential real-estate values.

East Project 2

Planners prepared a second proposal by locating the motorway farther away, following the border of the city, between the outer districts and the neighbouring suburban communes. However, no decision was made during the last years of the communist regime.

East Project 3

Two suburban communes insisted on building the motorway to the east of their territory. This new route is longer but cheaper than the second project, because it does not require by-passing Budapest Airport with a tunnel. Actually, these suburban communes have large areas for development in the east, whereas the second proposal would have been favourable for the outer districts.

The ambitious Mayor of the suburban commune of Gyál initiated an association of neighbouring settlements to develop non-governmental pressure. The outer districts of the city also had their associations. Since a compromise seemed impossible to find, the Ministry of Transport and Communication suspended the financing of the eastern section in 1993 and switched to the northern part.

North Project

The northern and north-western section would first of all serve Budapest and the elite suburbs (some hilly and forested, some under environmental protection). The suggested motorway construction provoked harsh resistance, mostly from environmental associations. The environmentally acceptable solution would require the construction of long tunnels, which would raise the costs excessively.

Towards a Metropolitan Compromise

The municipalities along the suspended eastern section recognised that they had suffered serious losses, when they saw the booming development along the already finished portion. They then started to look for a compromise. In early 1998, the Minister of Transport and Communication, the Mayor of Budapest and the President of the Pest County Local Government accepted the East Project 3 proposal made by the suburban communes (see Figure 6.2). This agreement was later approved by the City Council, as well as by the outer district association. Infrastructure to facilitate intra-urban traffic, such as the construction of urban expressways, will be financed by the City of Budapest.

During the last decade, practically every planned section of the motorway provoked resistance, mainly for environmental reasons, sometimes over financial concerns. Environmental associations, sometimes unintentionally, supported one or another business interest group, as did — not always unintentionally — local governments too. It was a significant achievement to reach a consensus with regard to the very important south-eastern section.

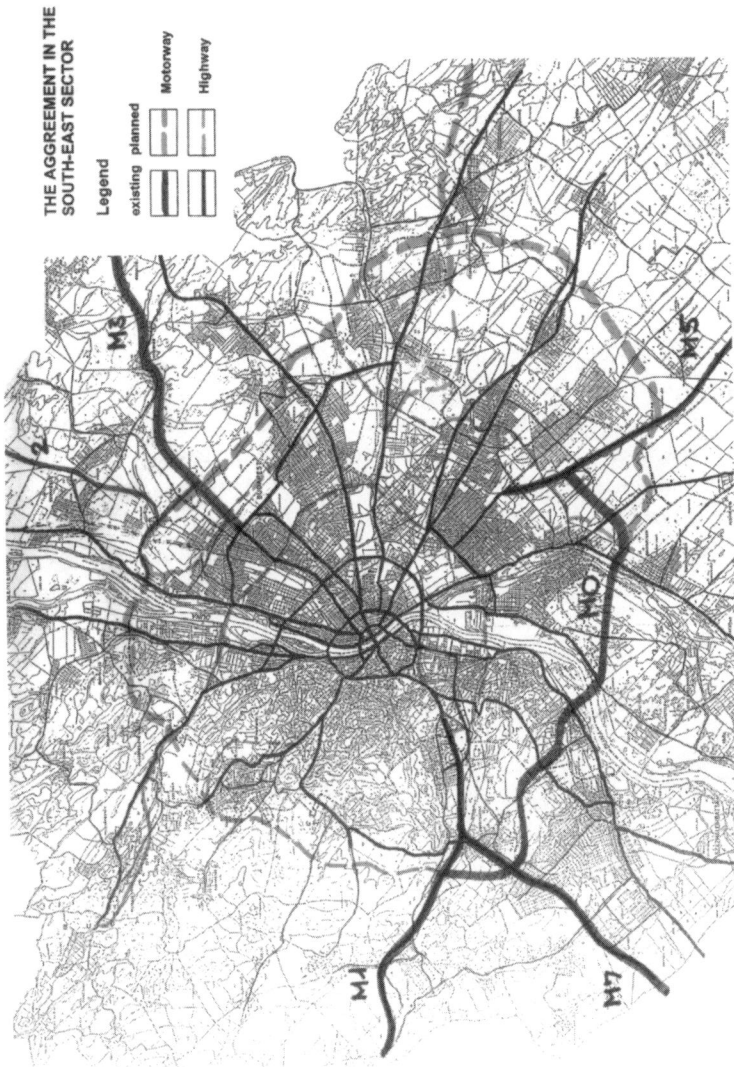

Figure 6.2 **The Budapest M0 Motorway Compromise:** *the South-east agreement*

The fate of the northern part is still uncertain. The bargaining process should be accelerated because the new Metropolitan Master Plan
— which should contain the motorway ring — will be presented to
Parliament by the end of 1999.

Consensus Building Process: A Failure or a Success?

The long consensus-building process was a failure for the planners, who had to modify their original plans several times. It was also a failure for the developers, as the ring road consists only of non-interrelated portions. Even the success of the protesting municipalities is doubtful, because they continue to suffer from traffic congestion, and the real-estate market along the blocked sections has become frozen.

Nevertheless, it was meaningful that civic movements were able to force the authorities to modify their original plans. It was quite exceptional that Budapest accepted the interests of two suburban communes, and did not use its dominating force. It was a very important learning process for the planners: they had to draw the lesson that technical optimisation is not enough for infrastructure development — the projects should also be socially acceptable. It was a valuable — and so far unique — experience for all the participants in the discussion: how to reach consensus among partners with conflicting interests.

6.4 Transport Infrastructure Impacts on Urban Life in Geneva

from Antoine S. Bailly, *"Large Transport Infrastructures and Quality of Life"*

Research on Transport and Quality of Life

A research project conducted in Geneva has aimed at analysing the interactions between urban development, transport infrastructures and the quality of urban life. It has consisted in analysing and evaluating the consequences of the creation and the use of large transport infrastructures for the localisation of economic activities (services, industries, etc.).

The following *three constitutive systems of urban space* have been considered:
- *the transport system* into which are inserted large transport infrastructures. This system is made up of all the elements linked to urban traffic flows — from the public transport network to all traffic in the city;
- *the system of localisation of activities* that reflects the spatial transformations induced by the transport system, as well as the changes in the distribution of jobs and housing, both from the physical point of view and from that of human perception;
- *the system of social relations* that shows the socio-spatial functioning of the city and appears at the level of urban practices (i.e. the mobility behaviour of city dwellers).

These systems are managed by different stakeholders who do not have the same logic of action and for whom large transport infrastructures do not have the same interest. When analysing the systems jointly, it becomes possible to understand and to discover the transformations induced by new transport opportunity and the expectations of the stakeholders about the transport infrastructure.

To analyse dynamic situations in a structural context, the joint analysis of the three constitutive systems requires a cross-cutting appreciation of the transport infrastructure impacts. The following *three stages* have to be taken into account:
- the *conception* and the period before the realisation of a transport infrastructure project (historical background, debates, votes, oppositions, etc.);
- the *realisation* of the project (construction, diffusion through economic activity);
- the transport infrastructure *use* and the *consequences* for the user and the non-user (advantages and disadvantages to the users, modification of practices, nuisances, etc.).

This cross-cutting analysis has to be conducted *at different geographical scales* (neighbourhood, city, region, metropolis) to appreciate the global impact of the transport infrastructure on urban development. Indeed, as large transport infrastructures connect territories, a new transport facility may have the various *repercussions on urban development* for one or more neighbourhoods, communes (see Figure 6.3), cities, cantons or regions. For example:

- urban centres or development nodes appear or lose importance;
- new growth potential or qualitative improvement appear;
- new mobility behaviours are engendered and thus favour new distributions of population and/or activities;
- important environmental impacts (noise, pollution) reduce quality of life.

Urban Policy Implications

Large transport infrastructure projects cannot be undertaken without public intervention. The research findings highlight how these projects represent an opportunity for local communities to influence the way land-use evolves. A fundamental step is an analysis of how public stakeholders use the regulatory mechanisms they have developed and codified to manage this type of project. The findings also refer to the question of governance, that is to the relationship between civic society and the political and administrative structures erected by the State.

In contrast to traditional urban projects, the decisions necessary for the elaboration of a large transport infrastructure project require the intervention of several institutional levels (the commune (s), canton (s), even the Confederation and/or equivalent political bodies for cross-border projects).

User interest groups may support a new infrastructure project that would reduce the time needed to get to work from where they live, while resident interest groups are opposed to it because of the barrier effect it would create.

Great care must be taken in the analysis of the decision-making processes that govern the emergence of the project, because they fits into the history and process of complex urban development. That is why the Geneva research has focused on the perceptions of the different stakeholders, and particular attention has been given to the public sector.

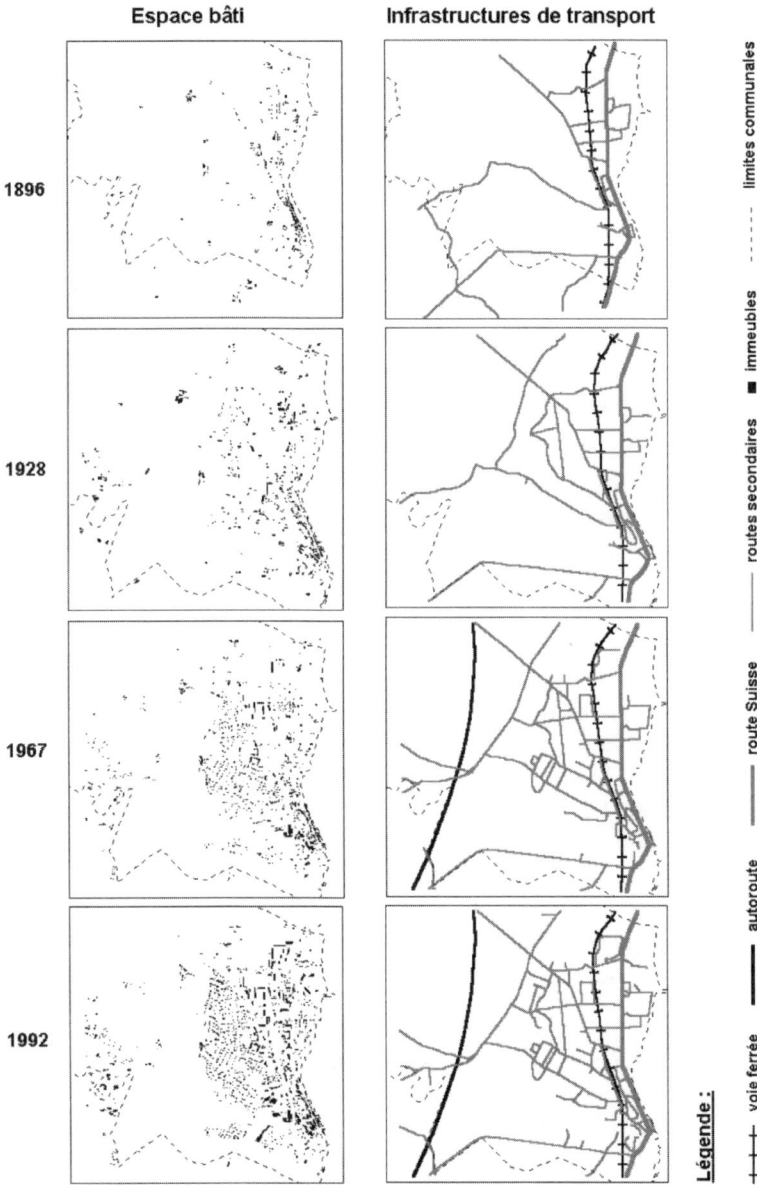

Source: Bailly (1998) p. 30

Figure 6.3 *Evolution of the Built Environment and Transport Infrastructure in Versoix, Geneva: in 1897 and 1992*

The research has reached the following conclusions:

- there are conflicting perceptions of the functions assigned to the large infrastructure networks;
- it is difficult to harmonise the know-how of experts and the knowledge of ordinary people;
- the way in which the potential of an infrastructure project is perceived and developed is strongly correlated to factors that go beyond the scope of the project (the importance of the economic context; pressure from the environmental protection lobby; land-use policy on concentrated development to preserve non-built areas).

Towards a New Planning Approach

In Switzerland until the 1980s, the creation of large-scale infrastructure followed a deductive logic: when transport problems arose, new projects were developed to improve the situation.

Since the 1980s, the communes, the cantons and citizen interest groups have made much more use of their power of objection. This evolution has determined an inductive logic, with co-ordination between project partners in a "culture of negotiation."

The example of the Geneva motorway bypass is an illustration of these co-ordination difficulties between European, federal, cantonal and communal levels. Projects have faced a series of objections, resulting in blockages and route changes. The negotiation and anticipation learning processes remains to be developed within a greater culture of co-ordination.

Recognising the Dual Effects of Transport Infrastructure

Transport infrastructures either connect or divide urban areas, qualify or disqualify public spaces, according to a geometry of urban fragmentation. Large-scale transport infrastructures not only have impacts near at hand but also at a distance. These effects are not just limited to traffic flows, but have repercussions even on such aspects as the localisation of activities and housing, and the mingling or segregation of populations. They also stimulate the emergence of new centres and new peripheries. Cities are at the same time fragmented by infrastructures and more accessible than before these were built.

Further Reading

Bailly, A., Bornicchia F., Müller R., Schlegel R. and Widmer G. (1998) *Grandes infrastructures de transport, forme urbaine et qualité de vie*, COST-C2 Rapport final, Genève : Université de Genève.

Bailly, A. and Widmer G. (1998) *"Grandes infrastructures et environnement urbain."* *Espace et sociétés* 95, 61-79.

Cape Metropolitan Council (1998) *"Moving Ahead"*, *Cape Metropolitan Transport Plan*. Cape Town: CMC.

Godard, X. and Teurnier, P. (1992) *"Caractéristiques des entreprises d'autobus africaines."* In *Les transports urbains en Afrique à l'heure de 1'ajustement*. Paris : Institut National de Recherches sur les Transports et leur Securité (INRETS).

Hiler, D. (1993) *"Et pourtant elle contourne."* Le réseau autoroutier genevois à l'épreuve de la démocratie. Genève : Département des travaux public du canton de Genève.

Newman, P. and Kenworthy, J. (1999) *Sustainability and Cities: overcoming automobile dependence*. Washington DC: Island Press.

Lefèvre, C. and Offner, J.-M. (1990) *Les transports urbains en question : usages, décisions, territoires*. Paris : Celse.

Ministère de l'aménagement du territoire, de l'équipement et des transports (1996) *Projet d'infrastructures et débat public*. Paris : Techniques, territoires et sociétés 31.

Pellegrino, P. et alii (1998), *"Infrastructures et modèles urbanstiques."* *Espaces et Sociétés*, 95, 9-31.

CHAPTER 7

Economic revitalisation

REVIVING THE LOCAL ECONOMY

In a sustainable approach to urban development, the city ought to be interpreted as an economic resource. It is a product of wealth, and its interacting stakeholders, as well as material and nonmaterial elements, are wealth producers. Beyond the purely functionalist perspective, this vision of the city is dependant on the determination of local partners and on the local resources that are to be managed. In this context, employment policies ought to be defined with due consideration to the potential of the production system. However, the reality is often different, as, for instance, when employment opportunities are linked to the presence of multinational companies: these follow purely economic interests and can close down their operations overnight.

The opportunities to maintain and attract employment on a sustainable basis are linked to a dynamic and open urban context. The sets of policies described in the previous sections contributes to this dynamism, because there cannot be economic development without quality public services or infrastructure provision. The "milieu theory" highlights the importance of local attractiveness. However, for many city authorities, dealing with unemployment constitutes a major constraint on local promotion.

Recent economic trends challenge existing development zones. Employment measures, in particular, require permanent innovative skills which city authorities do not usually have on their own. Some have favoured the establishment of platforms in which the private sector, educational, social and political stakeholders work together according to agreed principles to define projects. This approach has been applied in cities like Toronto, Cape Town or Lyon to face issues related to globalisation processes. With comparative advantages, each city has tried to find a role and purpose in the world system, based on local resources and conditions. Promotion policies are then proposed within this framework.

METROPOLITAN AND NEIGHBOURHOOD ECONOMIC DEVELOPMENT

In **Cape Town**, local authorities have been given more responsibility for economic development. Stewart Fisher discusses the potential of a planning framework which aims at integrating economic policy with environmental considerations, as well as objectives for promoting social harmony and reducing poverty. Such an approach is crucial for the Cape Metropole: *"while the Cape Metropolitan Area economy has had growth rates and skill levels that are significantly higher than the national average during the past decade, the challenge still lies in ensuring that the population as a whole benefits from economic development. In this regard the reduction of unemployment is a critical challenge."*

The aim of Cape Metropolitan Council is *"to develop and implement a holistic framework for addressing economic growth and poverty alleviation."* The policy basis for achieving this goal is the *Economic Development Framework* (see Chapter 7.1)

Making the Cape metropolitan area more competitive is one of the objective of the *Economic Development Framework*. *"The aim is to strengthen our economic position and create an attractive investment climate through, among others, the development of entrepreneurial skills, the promotion of tourism, regenerating and supporting strong integrating cultural life and improving safety and security."*

The policy implementation process envisaged for the plan is also innovative. *"The framework seeks to operate through a process of facilitation as opposed to intervention."* This process is presented as a key factor for the long-term success of the metropolitan development strategy.

In **Lyon**, social and economic disparities in the metropolitan area have forced local authorities to set priority policies in order to redress the balance, and re-skill the deprived neighbourhoods at the periphery of the city (see Chapter 7.2). Bruno Voisin stresses that physical improvements and employment measures have shown their limits and that, today, emphasis is on neighbourhood management and on "self-governance."

Participatory programmes have been developed with the objective to re-forge social links. These experiences show that *"maintaining social links goes hand-in-hand with respecting the environmental balance, pursuing economic development and controlling urban sprawl as one of the most important of the conurbation's policy areas."*

This participatory approach is part of a conurbation-wide policy framework. It recognises that *"the need to rejuvenate the large local-authority housing areas and let their inhabitants play a full role in the economic and cultural development of the urban area is the same as the need to ensure sustainable development by halting the factors that have caused imbalance and fragmentation within the metropolitan area."*

While recognising the impact of neighbourhood participatory projects, the author also stresses the "instigator" role of the State as a key factor to redress economic imbalances.

7.1   Economic Growth and Poverty Alleviation in Cape Town

from Stewart Fisher, *"Integrated Development Planning in the Cape Metropolitan Area"*

The Economic Development Framework Project

The new local government legislative framework gives municipalities the responsibility for economic development: local authorities have to promote and protect the economic health of the metropolitan area. The *Economic Development Framework* (EDF) was initiated by the Cape Metropolitan Council (CMC) to develop and implement a holistic framework for addressing economic growth and poverty alleviation and to promote sustainable urban development. The project was planned for formal launching in 1999.

Linkages with the Integrated Development Plan Themes

The EDF targets the five key themes of the *Integrated Development Plan* (see Chapter 2.4 for details). The framework contributes to the following objectives:

Targeting Poverty and Homelessness

The EDF will firstly address the issue of poverty by facilitating a working definition of, and approach to, poverty. Anti-poverty strategies that are integrated and co-ordinated will be developed. Comprehensive poverty audits will then be conducted. The understanding of how the poor survive will be central to the EDF, so as to ensure a direct complementarity between such practices and pro-active strategies.

An *Economic Trends and Spatial Patterns Study* launched in 1997 investigates areas of economic growth, and thus provides guidelines for the future location of housing and other development.

Strengthening the Cape Metropole's Global Economic Position

The changes taking place in the global economy have impacts on Cape Metropole industries and the very fabric of society. The nature of these impacts have to be understood in order to respond proactively to them. It is also necessary to understand that these impacts threaten some industries but, at the same time, offer enormous opportunities to other sectors. By positioning its industries, Cape Metropole becomes globally competitive. This cannot be done without a comprehensive metropolitan-wide strategy to alleviate poverty. Furthermore, areas of economic activity must be defined where the Cape Metropole could have either a competitive advantage or a natural market.

Enhancing the Environment

Central to the EDF is the development of programmes to ensure that the natural environment is protected and preserved for future generations. Where degradation has occurred, programmes are to be implemented for the restoration of the indigenous environment.

Building Social Harmony and Civic Responsibility

It is important to ensure that all communities in the Cape Metropole have access to the areas of opportunities and share in its prosperity. Furthermore it is essential to address the causes and effects of poverty and economic exclusion.

Developing Local Government

The EDF aims to ensure efficient use of scarce local authorities resources and to streamline development processes, especially with regard to the implementation of projects. The CMC should improve the delivery of services through the development of service culture and customer satisfaction.

Emerging Issues

The *Economic Development Framework* recognises the contradictions inherent in making cities globally competitive, whilst at the same time initiating major poverty reduction programmes. The EDF seeks to support the development of these activity areas (those that have either a competitive advantage or a natural market) through leverage and enablement. In this regard the framework seeks to operate through a process of facilitation as opposed to intervention. This has two advantages. The first is that it provides a much closer linkage between policy and implementation, which allows it to span the *IDP* themes more effectively. The second is that it mobilises existing resources, and thereby reduces its dependency upon external financial inputs. Both of these are important factors in the assessment of the potential for long-term success.

Economic Strengthening Through the Other CMC Projects

The Metropolitan Spatial Development Framework

The spatial development plan for the Cape Metropole provides an expectation of focused and committed public sector investment strategies, and hence confidence for both short- and long-term private investment strategies (see Chapter 5.1 for details).

Moving Ahead

Cape Metropole's global economic position is to be strengthened by providing adequate and well-maintained transport networks for the distribution of goods. Development potentials include: the port and airport; public transport links to the major tourist destinations; an efficient, effective, safe and affordable public transport system (see Chapter 6.2 for details).

Housing Needs Analysis

The delivery of housing will boost the construction industry, with ripple effects in numerous directions. An added benefit in this regard is that housing can be constructed with materials that are readily available. There are thus no costly imports. If the execution of the housing strategy occurs effectively, in terms of the correct location of housing and at adequate densities, then the urban economy is bound to perform more efficiently.

Environmental Policy

Tourism has become a major contributor to the economy of the Cape Metropole, and the region's environmental assets (both the natural and built/cultural environment, see Figure 7.1) underpin this growth industry. In order to continue to attract the tourists, an integrated environmental strategy for the Cape Metropole should ensure the sustainability of these assets.

Photo: DAEL, Geneva

Figure 7.1 **The Economic Importance of Cape Town's Environmental Assets:** *the conservation or protection of the region's striking vistas, of the urban edge, of sites of cultural and architectural significance, of the biodiversity, the upgrading and maintenance of the river and wetland systems — all are central elements of an environmental policy needed to ensure a sustainable management of Cape Town's tourism assets*

7.2   Re-skilling Lyon's Disadvantaged Neighbourhoods

from Bruno Voisin, *"Social Development and Local Governance in Greater Lyon"*

Redressing the Balance in Disadvantaged Neighbourhoods

Uneven urban development and social imbalance over the last 30 years in Lyon have had grave consequences from the point of view of social equilibrium, disparities within the city, and for the urban environment (see Chapter 2.5 for details). This is why the Lyon Urban Community has instigated a set of priority policies during the 1990s on the re-skilling of areas of local-authority housing and maintaining a balance in bringing in new populations. This is directly linked to other areas of urban planning, including housing and urban transportation; the protection of the environment; the avoidance of urban sprawl; and the development of the Lyon Urban Region.

Maintaining social links therefore goes hand-in-hand with respecting the environmental balance, pursuing economic development and controlling urban sprawl, as one of the most important conurbation policy areas.

From Physical Improvements to Self-governance

Within the framework of a *City Contract*, 23 major neighbourhoods were earmarked for priority action. These areas are mainly situated in the inner ring of the east side of the conurbation, where industrial growth and the development of local-authority housing made their mark in the 1960s and 1970s. They have become increasingly disadvantaged both socially and economically (see Figure 7.2).

Overall action in these neighbourhoods includes the revamping of buildings; the development of public spaces and local environmental improvements; a greater commitment to get people back to work and involved in the local economy; also to help people of immigrant origin to integrate and to reduce crime.

These urban projects are part of an *overall conurbation scheme* which aims to improve life in the "priority" neighbourhoods and to establish a conurbation-wide policy, particularly in relation to housing and transport.

At the same time, *Local Programmes for Economic Integration* subsidised by the European Union aim to involve people margina-lised through social change in new opportunities in Greater Lyon.

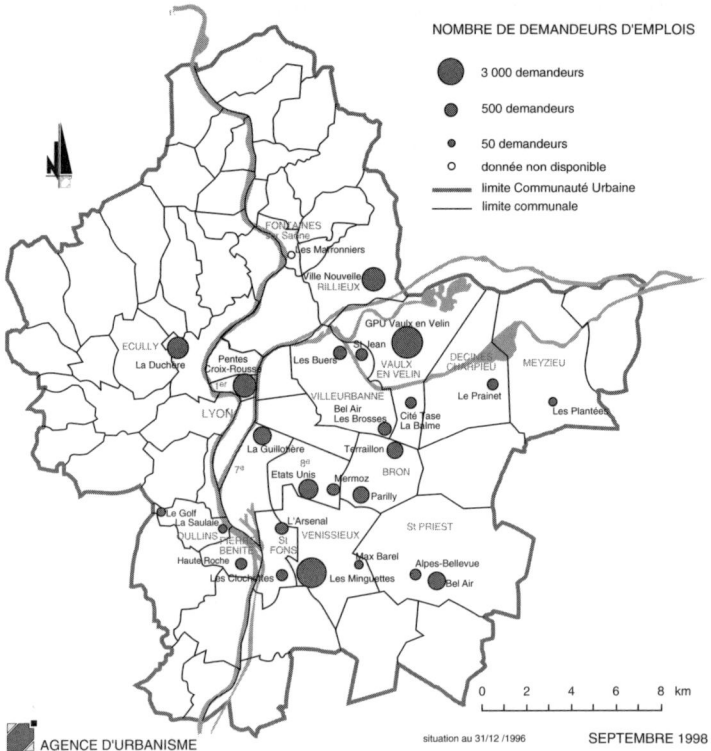

NOMBRE DE DEMANDEURS D'EMPLOIS

- 3 000 demandeurs
- 500 demandeurs
- 50 demandeurs
- ○ donnée non disponible
- ▬ limite Communauté Urbaine
- ── limite communale

0   2   4   6   8 km

AGENCE D'URBANISME   situation au 31/12 /1996   SEPTEMBRE 1998

Source: Communauté Urbaine de Lyon, Agence d'Urbanisme pour le Développement de l'Agglomération Lyonnaise (1998) p. 6

Figure 7.2 **Unemployment in the Disadvantaged Urban Areas of Greater Lyon in 1996**

Every year the Urban Community invests almost FRF 100 million on high-priority zones. Until recently, investments were allocated for the renovation of housing, restructuring open spaces and setting up additional services. Today, emphasis is on the day-to-day running of the neighbourhood and on self-governance: getting people to be responsible for the running of their local area and its facilities.

For a period of almost ten years Lyon has formulated a genuine development policy, based on a balanced conurbation-wide approach, and also concerning the day-to-day lives of those in the most disadvantaged areas.

A Role for Both Local Governance and State Support

A reduction in the negative impacts of unemployment, job insecurity and antagonism between different social or local groups of people in the disadvantaged neighbourhoods cannot be achieved solely through routine local-authority decisions. Formal consultation with residents about their needs and expectations is not enough, nor is the backing of association leaders, social workers and resident volunteers.

In order to stop people being excluded from playing an active role in their community, authorities need to instigate voluntary-based initiatives to help community improvement projects, taking all aspects of the situation — social, urban, economic and cultural — into account. These initiatives enable the residents to come forward and become an active force in bettering their own situation.

The experience of Lyon shows the importance of the instigator role of the State: to define an overall framework and flexible forms of contracting that allow the various authorities to get involved; to launch the debate on individual responsibilities and define how action can be taken with respect to direct or indirect financial support for programmes. In particular, the State has to define the nature of assistance or incentives that it could provide, such as the transfer of funds to local authorities, the introduction of tax exemption measures, or supporting local investments.

Participatory Initiatives for Economic Revitalisation

Amongst measures for youth employment, several neighbourhoods have appointed a young "head of communications" whose responsibility is to create opportunities for dialogue in the community. These are young people working voluntarily who often come from the neighbourhoods themselves and can communicate with their own age group. Older teenagers and young adults can be those who suggest the most dynamic development projects, especially those of a cultural nature.

Other initiatives such as the *Residents' Envoys, Neighbourhood Councils* and *Neighbourhood Corporations* constitute innovative participatory frameworks to involve the residents (see Chapter 2.5 for details). On a economic perspective, they allow:
- the general promotion of the neighbourhood and getting young people into work;
- residents' involvement in improving their environment and developing local services within their neighbourhood; re-forging the social links in an area blighted by poverty and social exclusion by involving those residents who are most disadvantaged and who have suffered most with unemployment in looking after their urban environment;
- the remuneration for full- or part-time work maintaining the communal parts of buildings and outside spaces, participating in

work to make improvements and helping set up new services. Such remuneration can really help an individual or family in financial difficulty. It might also be the first work experience gained by a school leaver, or it might enable a long-term unemployed person to be reintroduced into the work-force.

These participatory initiatives contribute to redistributing spending power for the benefit of a poor population living in a socially segregated area. They constitute a genuine tool of economic development, helping create new commercial facilities.

Further Reading

Bailly, A. and Huriot, J.M. (eds.) (1999) *Villes et croissance*. Paris: Anthropos.

Communauté Urbaine de Lyon, Agence d'urbanisme (1998) *Observatoire des territoires sensibles*. Rapport annuel. Lyon: AUDAL.

Delbos, V. and Jacquier, C. (1997) *Développement économique, emploi et revitalisation des quartiers en crise*. Saint Denis: D.I.V.

Hatzfeld, H., Hatzfeld, M., and Ringart, N. (1998) *Quand la marge est créatrice: les interstices urbains, initiateurs d'emploi*. La Tour d'Aigues: Éditions de l'Aube

Hatzfeld, M. (1998) *Topo — Guide des régies de quartier: Tisser le lien social*. Paris: Desclée de Brouwer

Polèse, M. (1994) *Economie urbaine et régionale*. Paris: Economica.

Collective (Journal). (1996) *"Des habitants créateurs d'activités économiques: des dynamiques en émergence."* Les Cahiers du CR DSU 10 (March), Lyon.

Collective (Journal). (1997) *"Les services publics entre adaptation et territorialisation."* Les Cahiers du CR.DSU 17 (Dec.), Lyon.

Collective (Journal). (1997) *"Gestion de proximité, gestion territorialisée."* Les Cahiers du CRDSU 16 (May), Lyon.

Wuhl, S. (1996) *Insertion: les politiques en crise*. Paris: P.U.F

CHAPTER 8

Towards a model of socially sustainable urban development

> *"Today more than ever, urban authorities are facing the challenge to act in an efficient way, despite uncertain economic circumstances. Nevertheless, nobody can decide without integrating the consequences of choices and without bringing in the whole range of urban stakeholders who have an impact on their collective destiny. The responsibility and legitimacy of urban authorities are dependent on their ability to manage the future of cities."* [1]

The varied policies implemented in those cities participating in the UNESCO-MOST Project and outlined in the preceding chapters show that *"city management has a crucial role in facilitating social development."*[1] Much emphasis has been placed on governance, and particularly on the legislative and institutional frameworks required or established to manage metropolitan growth with social objectives.

Cities aim to frame their urban policies in a more sustainable perspective, giving thoughts to the interrelations between planning, economic considerations, and social problems. In Cape Town and Geneva, new institutional planning frameworks have been devised to improve the quality of metropolitan and regional management.

---

1 The quotations in this chapter are given without mention of the authors: they are transcriptions of open discussion taped during the Cape Town Colloquium or written suggestions made within the follow-up of the MOST Network.

Nairobi and San Salvador are committed to greater democracy, for a more inclusive system of governance engaging a wider social participation in the urban planning processes. In some Brazilian cities, participatory instruments have been devised to initiate, manage and finance social housing projects.

Social inequality issues are taking a more prominent place on the agenda of urban authorities. In Lyon for instance, participatory frameworks have been established to manage socially deprived neighbourhoods using partnerships. Immigration and inter-ethnic cohabitation issues are being considered with more positive public policies: social and cultural transformations of metropolitan neighbourhoods are monitored in Toronto; new strategies based on ethnic segmentation and accessibility are tried in Montreal. Other policies for socially sustainable urban development are tested elsewhere: improving the safety in the city of Milan; assessing urban housing quality in Geneva; focusing on social housing provision in Rotterdam; evaluating the impact of large transport infrastructures on the quality of life in Geneva.

These experiences point to common approaches about the ways in which municipalities engage in socially sustainable urban management. Cities acknowledge that urban problems have to be addressed at various geographical levels, and that it is necessary to integrate global and local policies. Strategies are being developed which recognise that urban management processes are complex and require concerted action from a whole range of stakeholders.

Stemming from informal discussions within the MOST Network, it is possible to point to new avenues for research and policy development on the social sustainability of cities.

First, the progress and future challenges for socially sustainable urban development are examined. A cross-cutting and comparative research agenda is then outlined, with several issues requiring further discussion to strengthen the social dimension in urban management policy and practice.

Networking on Social Sustainability in Cities

The aim of the MOST project on Socially Sustainable Cities is to build an internationallly comparable knowledge base for researchers and practitioners (see Chapter 1). It is appropriate to ask what progress has been made with regard to the main objectives defined, in particular regarding key local policy areas, spatial and social policy integration, urban policy comparison and good practice dissemination.

Concentrating on Key Local Policy Areas

The analysis of governance, of policies for social integration, housing, transport, public services, and for economic development has highlighted different experiences and perspectives on how cities are coping with key challenges of metropolitan management. Detailed case studies have illustrated how cities have attempted to integrate social objectives in urban management, and have succeeded or failed in this. This first step towards building a knowledge base on metropolitan development has provided some useful concepts and operative principles that are relevant for the promotion of social sustainability.

Stemming from these case studies, a series of cross-cutting themes have emerged. They include metropolitan governance; partnership; diversity; social equity; policy integration; complexity. These issues point to *"new global and positive ways of looking at the future of cities"* that ought to be explored further to develop social agendas for urban planning. These new research avenues are considered in more detail below.

Integrating the Spatial and Social Policy Perspectives

A number of linkages between social and spatial considerations have been examined: social consequences of urban planning decisions and spatial impacts of social policies. Urban research and policy development need to devote more attention to these links, as they are the main components of the complexity underlying the integrated management of cities.

Comparing Policy Experience

A fundamental research approach for sustainable urban management is to compare knowledge about the key factors which make local policies successful. Comparing cities in and across both the North and the South, and identifying policies and methodologies which could be transferred, has proven difficult: *"Comparisons of urban management experience are difficult to achieve because it is unlikely to find two cities that are facing the same challenges and which operate with the same legal and social framework. Processes are 80% sui generis, within the local context. There are many convincing cases, with similarities, but they are not replicas that can be reapplied in another city. Comparison will at the most give some ideas to improve the system."*

The experiences are also too varied and too heavily focused on precise cases to allow anyone to define convincing recommendations for a socially sustainable approach to urban management. *"Guidelines can offer useful conceptual direction, but are never perfect recommendations for the reality of the conditions and processes that are found in specific cities."*

Bearing in mind these limitations, it is useful too keep some comparative outlook of social urban policy and experience in the work of the MOST Network, as this approach is important to go beyond case studies, to make links and to promote conceptualisation.

Disseminating Good Practice

The dissemination of good practice is an overall aim of the MOST Project. The following issues are central for the successful transfer of knowledge and experience stemming from case studies.

- *Raise the right questions*

What problems were identified and what lessons have been learnt from the past?

- *Integrate the local urban context*

What elements were central to setting up a framework for action? Which values required consideration?

- *Define objectives for policy measures*

What priorities were formulated?

- *Define financial means und set up partnerships*

What budget was allocated for action? What co-operation processes were applied?

- *Evaluate the results*

What criteria were used to assess the quality of achievements? What solutions and/or new challenges evolved?

- *Define guidelines for urban authorities*

What is relevant for sustainable transferable urban policies?

Networking: A Wider Ability to Understand Alternatives

Connections between research and policy-making are happening. Several forums, including the MOST Network, bring together a mix of disciplines and professions to discuss, share and compare urban management experiences. Networking is also taking a new dimension with the development of communication technologies. For example, cities are able to find out on the Web what others are doing in the area of urban management and to position themselves as to what they should be doing themselves.

Connections are however often established within specific frameworks which are frequently not linked or do not allow easy access to findings. In addition, social and institutional processes are often so much within the local context that networking has limited outcomes in terms of policy development. *"Networks allow us to start a dialogue and to get relevant information, but they rarely offer the best model of what can be done."* Nevertheless, networking is a way to promote the debate on social sustainability and strengthen concerted action between research and policy.

Improving the connections between people working in the same field is a way *"to gain a wider ability to understand alternatives. Connecting the different parts of the urban forces is a new form of organisation to manage cities, which offers a lot more freedom to define alternatives for urban management than a hierarchical model."*

By networking, a wide range of social groups have opportunities to work laterally, to find out about similar experiences and to discuss them. *"This approach enables the implementation of new methods that are more multidisciplinary and operational. Above all, it is a very important basis for the new form of governance at the centre of the MOST debates, bringing civil society more in contact with government. Networking thus becomes an overarching model to describe the way cities operate."*

Developing Wide-ranging Connections

Wide-ranging connections ought to be developed to go beyond the objective of connecting researchers and policy-makers. *"The commitment to networking and to exchanging ideas on urban management should be present not only between policy and research, but also across disciplines and professions, working on operational and conceptual development."*

People who work on conceptual development have to bring their studies to the level at which there can be a response from those who work on the operational side, on the ground at the local level. *"The ultimate objective of networking is to enhance projects, to pull out what can be generalised, and to make connections with ideas or general trends going on elsewhere. Hence, practitioners are able to reinterpret their projects and researchers are incited to think how the general is interrelated to the particular."*

How can this interchange be promoted? *"Networking is occurring, but one must remain conscious of making the connections, because the exchange of knowledge often proves difficult."* In particular, there is insufficient systematic feedback information on project work: there are few publications on project evaluations, and practitioners are rarely invited sceintific meetings.

Links to other international programmes with mission statements and objectives similar to those of this UNESCO-MOST Project should also be developed, in particular *"projects dealing with urban development, such as the WHO Healthy City Project, the Habitat Agenda and the Local Agenda 21 Project."*

There is considerable scope for exchanges because, whereas many of these programmes focus on developing countries and national policies, this MOST Project concentrates on local management practices and involves cities in both the South and the North.

The UN *Best Practices and Local Leadership Programme* is one framework in which this type of link could be strengthened. This Programme is a network dedicated to the identification and exchange of innovative and successful solutions for sustainable development.

Example of an Operational Partnership

The partnership established between the Cape Metropolitan Council and the Canton of Geneva is an interesting example of an exchange based at the operational level (see Chapter 8.1). *"This type of networking experience constitutes a new way to try and understand how another public authority practises urban and regional planning for transport, housing, infrastructure and urbanisation. Such partnerships should be more common, as networking ought not to remain at the research level."*

8.1 A Partnership at the Operational Level between Geneva and Cape Town

by Philippe Brun, based on *"Partnership Framework Agreement"*

One of the aims of the MOST research project on Socially Sustainable Cities is to establish North-South links between cities that share comparable challenges and problems. To develop such links, the Cape Metropolitan Council (CMC) and the Canton of Geneva engaged in setting up a partnership.

During exploratory visits, a number of fields of common interest in land-use planning, urban development and management were defined. In 1997 and 1998, both political authorities accepted the principle of a partnership and designated the partner agencies: the Spatial Planning Department for the CMC, and the *Département de l'aménagement, de l'équipement et du logement* (DAEL) for the Canton of Geneva.

Common Concerns

The Cape Metropolitan Area and Geneva share a number of geographical and political characteristics, which have implied similar land-use planning, urban development and management approaches. These characteristics include the exceptional geographical site of these cities and their world-wide renown, far surpassing their actual size and role.

The CMC is to integrate several million people into its economy, while developing it and preserving its unique environment at the same time. It also has to be more in keeping with the cultural heritage of the new majority of its citizens.

Geneva is developing relations with the surrounding French region and has to integrate this new regional dimension into its urban planning. The economic and political centres have to be balanced, including those of the neighbouring Canton of Vaud. Cross-border management of urban planning and development need to be developed, in order to preserve the landscape and natural environment.

Aims of the Partnership

This partnership aims to explore the following practical fields:
- the macro-evaluation of strategic metropolitan projects;
- the densification of urban and suburban areas;
- sustainable development planning accounting for the environmental assets of the region;

- comparing, evaluating and complementing planning principles;
- organising and managing a Geographical Information System;
- linking specific macro-engineering projects and urban planning.

Guiding Principles

The partnership consists of an exchange of experienced professional staff between the two agencies. Participation of staff must be active, with hands-on involvement in partner work, in order to both communicate their own experience and expertise and to take advantage of their exposure to the planning and management activities of the partner city. Exchange visits are planned for three months.

Partnership Management

The agencies maintain close liaison to implement the partnership and define the scope of the missions. Each partner keeps their relevant authorities informed of the progress of the partnership, on a six-month or yearly basis.

After the initial exchange of staff, both parties will evaluate the advantages of a long-term partnership, and should the latter be continued, explore the possibility of establishing a Partnership Fund.

The First Exchange Visit Experience

In 1998, a staff member of the *Direction de l'aménagement* of the DAEL participated in the first three-month exchange with a posting at the CMC Spatial Planning Department. A report was prepared on the impact of mega-projects on the corridors/nodes development planned within the Cape Metropolitan Area development plan, the *MSDF* (see Chapter 5.1 for details). The report later constituted the basis of a workshop involving different urban stakeholders (planners, representatives of the business and transport sectors).

A working definition of the concept of "mega-project" was formulated. An evaluation grid was developed, considering notions such as the function, size, financial impact, implementation cost and metropolitan significance of the mega-projects.

The mission also included participation in technical advisory committee meetings, in presentations of planning studies and in discussions with municipality representatives.

In spite of the differences in scale and in socio-cultural context, the exchange showed convergence in planning approaches and work methods. It was an enriching opportunity for professional and personal development: facing up to new town planning practices; integrating into a team; adapting to problem definition and planning already underway; understanding another culture.

The Scope of the Next Exchange

The next phase of the partnership is the participation of a CMC staff member in an exchange visit to Geneva. The relevance of this interaction is the opportunity to undertake an in-depth analysis of Geneva's well-established built environment. Empirical lessons learnt will be of value to the application of the reconstruction and integration strategies embodied in the *MSDF*.

The suggested study topics concern the application of the following spatial development strategies on which the success of the *MSDF* depend greatly:
- urban densification strategies;
- urban integration and mixed land-use strategies;
- urban edge demarcation and management strategies.

Another possible study area is the relationship between the built environment (densities, uses and thresholds) and successful transport strategies.

Bridging Urban Contexts

The partnership is considered as a way to facilitate the MOST initiative, the primary purpose of which is to compare social and spatial transformations in emerging urban situations with that in mature urban contexts. The partnership is an opportunity for bridging established and emerging urban contexts. Hence it can play a role in sharing and reapplying knowledge and experience.

CROSS-CUTTING
AND COMPARATIVE RESEARCH AVENUES

Metropolitan governance, partnership, diversity, social equity, policy integration and complexity have emerged as cross-cutting issues prevalent in most areas of urban management, and requiring a wider debate. The approach to these themes have to emphasise the social and spatial linkages, and include comparative perspectives. It is also important to integrate both theory and practical policy considerations.

As a first step, the identified cross-cutting issues can be linked and analysed through the following three headings:
- focusing on metropolitan governance in partnership;
- dealing with diversity and aiming for social equity;
- addressing complexity and working towards policy integration.

These issues require a balanced approach. Some are under-researched and need to be theorised. Others require a practical examination rather than academic considerations. The different themes have to be examined with a *"healthy tension between theory and concrete examples or the immediate needs of policy."*

A three-stage approach is proposed to develop this new research agenda:
- descriptive work, illustrated with examples taken from case studies (including some comparative perspective with at least one other city);
- an analysis of the implications of the case studies for research, policy definition and implementation;
- a conceptual development of each cross-cutting issue.

In order to begin the debate on the identified cross-cutting issues, preliminary suggestions are outlined below (see Chapters 8.2, 8.3 and 8.4), on aspects which ought to be examined to strengthen the social agenda in urban management. These suggestions constitute possible avenues for research, and are meant to stimulate future analyses within the MOST Network or other networks.

8.2   Focusing on Metropolitan Governance in Partnership

An Under-theorised Concept

Urban governance is a central theme running through many case studies presented in the MOST Network. *"It is one of the most important institutional challenges that many cities face, and a principle which is branded everywhere. While there is a lot of descriptive work on the subject, the concept itself lacks theoretical development."* A critical analysis on a theoretical level ought to concentrate on how governance works, how it overlaps with, and is implemented by, partnerships.

Governance case studies have mainly emphasised the role of legislative and institutional reforms, but it should not overlook the *"non-permanent institutional frameworks: structures which evolve over time, and offer broader and adaptable frameworks for urban management."*

The Optimum Scale and Form of Governance

A recurring question for urban planning is to define what is the pertinent administrative *scale* at which urban management ought to be applied. The most appropriate scale of governance is a critical concern for sustainability, but no simple model can be defined. *"Is it just an administrative scale or also a geographic or a demographic scale? There is not just a single answer: it varies considerably from place to place and with the kind of problems that have to be dealt with."*

The question of the most appropriate *form* of urban governance also needs to be raised. Cities have to assess the various outcomes of a change of institutional framework. For instance, *"what is the feasibility of establishing a metropolitan government and what would its structure be? Which is the best way to achieve this goal: creating first a metropolitan institution or arriving at this after a long consensual process among the different urban actors? The first way prioritises the issue of the urban form of government; the second, the issue of developing urban governance relations."* A comparative analysis of governance relations in several cities could provide some answers to these questions, evaluate practices and help establish a general framework for policy development.

Emphasising the Role of Urban Stakeholders

Case studies also highlight the changing role of urban management and how it begins to contribute to social development. *"Cities act in a facilitating role, with a social agenda. This facilitation process is prevalent in all areas of activities discussed, in housing, transport, the integration process."* This major shift in urban management has to be explored, in order to understand the crucial role of political and administrative structures facilitating social development and spatial change in cities.

While urban authorities are key stakeholders, the role of the State is also critical in promoting socially sustainable cities. *"National policy can contribute to growing inequalities, for instance when the State looses its levelling function."* This *"vertical"* dimension has to be included in the thematic analysis of governance, to carefully monitor, for instance, the changes of State support policies.

Democratic Accountability and Efficiency

Community participation is one of the prerequisites for sustainable urban development. However, as described by Arnstein (1969), this concept can encompass a whole range of levels of participation, from manipulation, or tokenism to full empowerment with real citizen control.

To assess why participation has been more successful in certain projects than others, *"the tools and the methods that are available for involving different groups in the community have to be carefully examined. In order to have meaningful communication and negotiation with such a varied group of actors in the city, it is necessary to have a common language understood by all."*

What other elements are required to foster a real co-operation and negotiation between urban authorities and city dwellers? The consolidation of democratic control, the involvement of the private sector and NGOs clearly are ways to develop social and sustainable urban management in terms of accountability and efficiency.

8.3   Dealing with Diversity and Aiming for Social Equity

"Municipalities are beset with more and more social, economic and political challenges. However, focusing on the social side is crucial because social diversity is one of the hallmarks of cities: it unlocks a freedom, an ability to innovate, and openness specific to cities."

To strengthen socially sustainable urban development, public policies have to address issues of diversity and social equity. How can urban diversity, for instance, be considered as a positive force? Studies in Montreal show that policies for a pluralist city offer possible alternatives to social and cultural integration. How can social equity be promoted in planning policies? In particular, social policy areas such as, for instance, health or safety, have to be added to the agenda that promotes social equity.

Harnessing Social and Cultural Diversity

The negative aspects of social and cultural diversity often receive much attention, whereas the positive elements are rarely recognised. The importance of social diversity, described as one of the *"hallmarks of cities,"* requires that urban stakeholders *"understand how to maintain diversity on the streets and harness it in a positive way."*

The positive approach to social and cultural diversity is already present in the Harris model for a poly-nuclear city (Harris and Ullman, 1945), with several services, social and cultural nodes within or around a city. The positive impacts of social and cultural diversity can take on many forms. As illustrated by the example of the week-long Caribbean carnival in Toronto: *"The Caribbean Parade was first considered with mistrust for fear of violence. This event held each year, however, not only promotes social interaction among ethnic groups but also brings thousands of visitors and yields millions in tax revenue to the city."*

The Pluralist Metropolis

Alternative policy approaches to deal with cultural diversity also have to be compared and assessed. The issue of inter-ethnic cohabitation in a metropolitan area can be approached with four questions:
- *"What is required to avoid exclusion and segregation and, more generally, urban fragmentation?*
- *Are social and ethnic mix and socio-economic integration unavoidable objectives for urban management?*

- *Are they realistic objectives?*
- *Do they insure urban cohesion, one of the basic requirements for a socially sustainable city?"*

A comparative analysis of conurbations (Toronto, Vancouver, Paris) has been undertaken to explore the following two areas:
- the conditions for a successful neighbourhood life in multi-ethnic districts;
- the conditions for a city centre with liveable social and economic functions.

"Both neighbourhood life and the socio-economic dynamics of city centres have to be considered to meet the challenge of cohabitation in a "pluralist metropolis."" The hypothesis is that, as in Montreal, *"the relative lack of cohabitation at the neighbourhood level might be counter-balanced by an integrating city centre where the different groups meet and mix, despite the rather homogenous existing districts. Or, referring to the old English saying, " good fences make good neighbours.""*

Promoting Social Equity Policies

The concept of "equity planning" refers to *"planning efforts that pay particular attention to the needs of the poor and vulnerable populations, populations also likely to suffer the burdens of racial and sexual discrimination, both institutional and personal"* (Krumholz and Forester, 1990). Equity planning involves actions in different areas, including *"economic equity, equity of opportunity and access, equity of results and public services delivery, and cultural equity"* (Blakely, Fallon and Hoffman, 1995).

These definitions show the relevance of social equity as a sensitive dimension of urban sustainability. Social equity is also seen as *"a core principle and a conceptual. challenge for both research and policy making"*; *"a premise and an implicit goal for most people working in the field of social development, but one that we all need to be more conscious of."* Those multiple dimensions of social equity and examples of policy implementation need to be assessed with particular regard to their impact on the quality of life in cities.

Putting Health into the Urban Agenda

Health issues have sometimes been overlooked by urban management policy and ought to be given more careful attention. The incidence of diverse forms of ill health remains associated, in many parts of the world, with place of residence. In addition, increasing rates of delinquency, crime and violence have reduced residents' sense of security.

Unemployment, homelessness and social exclusion are experienced by the poor, ethnic minorities, female-headed households and refugees. There is growing evidence that these problems are associated with health and well-being inequalities. Finally, some characteristics of the built environment can hinder mobility, promote segregation and restrict health promotion of children, the elderly and handicapped persons. *"These situations indicate that health ought to be on the policy agenda that promotes social sustainability."* This is one of the objectives of the WHO's "Healthy Cities" Project. *"Current debate suffers from conceptual misunderstandings and lack of information. In order to overcome the shortcomings and integrate health promotion into research and policy agendas, discussions must focus on the inadequacies of current economic, public education, housing and urban planning policies for promoting health and well-being."*

Putting Urban Safety into the Agenda

Safety in cities is another neglected issue of the urban management debate, one that also has implications for community life. *"Urban violence is rapidly becoming one of the major problems of urban areas throughout the world. It seriously threatens the quality of daily life in the city and produces the well known phenomenon of retrenchment of the wealthier classes into "bunker cities"."*

Roderick Lawrence (1999) describes how *"apart from the costs of damage to, or loss of property, policing and criminal justice, crimes have many negative impacts on urban communities, including the insecurity of perceived high risks, fear, and victimisation. Research has identified a high correlation between geographical incidence of criminal offences and economic and social indicators of disadvantage and poverty. [...] Moreover, traditional measures to counteract delinquency, crime and violence have not been effective."*

In many countries specific urban safety policies have been developed, which concern justice, police and social interventions. However, *"these policies do not take into account the physical organisation of the city, and what is worse, they are generally not integrated into the physical reality of the urban structure."*

"The physical structure of buildings, housing estates, urban sectors is not a determinant of behaviour, but spatial patterns do have an influence on human behaviour. Transferred to safety we can say that careful design and planning of the physical space of the city do not guarantee a safe environment, but they contribute to it. Conversely, poor physical organisation generates lack of safety." Aspects of spatial organisation have to be developed in urban safety policy.

8.4   Addressing Complexity and Co-ordinating Policy

An Underlying Complexity

The complexity of urban management underlies most policy areas, as illustrated by the many forms that governance can take, as well as the challenging goals of dealing with urban diversity and of promoting social equity.

"*Research projects should explicitly address the issue of complexity and make links to the theoretical and methodological body of literature on this subject. Research should explore, for instance, how architecture and urban planning have in the past ignored diversity and complexity, creating many of the present urban problems.*" Although there is some consensus among the many specialists involved with urban planning and building, there are also inconsistencies and conflicts that hinder the formulation for integrative perspectives and the application of co-ordinated approaches.

The formulation and implementation of traditional sectoral approaches in housing, and in town and country planning has not led to optimal results. Incremental improvements (in sectors such as employment, housing or transport) are often achieved in tandem with unintended consequences, which may include negative impacts on the environmental conditions in cities, the economy, the health and well-being of citizens. In part, these mixed outcomes are also to the recurrent lack of environmental and social policies in the field of urban planning, which Lawrence (1995) notes "*can be associated with the following facts:*

- *The number and the complexity of all those factors that researchers, practitioners and policy decision-makers ought to consider.*
- *The uncertainties and the unpredictability of the interrelations between many of these factors.*
- *The segmented knowledge of researchers, public administrators and practitioners who may be experts on specific subjects but who do not have an integrated perspective of what they consider.*
- *The lack of co-ordination between actors in different sectors and between people working at different administrative levels.*
- *The lack of systematic monitoring and feedback within sectors (such as housing or transport) and especially across different local, regional and national levels.*
- *The non-account of goals, priorities and values which are related to the ways policy decision-makers and citizens*

*develop local economies, interpret and use human settlement
and value the qualities of its habitat."*

In order to rethink the way cities are planned, a fundamental question has to be addressed: *"Are inadequate responses to social, economic, health and environmental problems due to a lack of knowledge, or an inability to effectively use acquired knowledge, or to other circumstance? In other terms are we concerned with problems of substance, or procedures, or both?"*

Considering policy time frames is another aspect of the complexity of urban management. *"We must remain conscious that ecological, social and economic problems do not necessarily have compatible frameworks: some require short-term strategies, others long-term objectives."* These complex time frames are essential dimensions of urban management.

The importance of social identity also has to be highlighted. It needs to be integrated into spatial planning considerations. *"The growing social and spatial inequalities in metropolitan areas have negative impacts on social esteem and self-esteem. They raise further questions about the claims and responsibilities of groups in metropolitan areas with respect to our social value systems and social identity."*

Several research areas are outlined in the following sections, which are avenues to improve current understanding of the multiple and interrelated spatial, social and economic dimensions of urban policy making.

Integrated Approaches in Research and Policy Development

The formulation of co-ordinated approaches is necessary to acknowledge the complexity of urban management, to understand the links between the spatial, economic and social aspects of urban policies.

Research needs to get *"a much better view of the relationship between the spatial transformations of cities and the impact of those changes have on the people who live in the cities."* What are are, for instance, the consequences of another recent shift in urban management — the important political and economic changes that have occurred over the last ten years? *"With the dominance of the market-driven society on economies at the local level, cities no longer have either the finance, the capability, or perhaps the political will to intervene physically in the way that was done before."*

Social Appropriation of Urban Projects

The acceptance of urban projects by the local population is a sensitive issue for the social sustainability of cities. Placing major infrastructures projects in deprived urban neighbourhoods is a planning policy that raises opposing views of their social impact. Are such policy decisions based on social equity? Do these infrastructures attract more diverse people into deprived areas? Is it sufficient to speak about social integration?

The Stadium of France, built in the Saint-Denis district in the deprived suburbs of Paris, is an example of such a planning decision. For some, this development has been *"a way to promote a new urban culture"*, *"an opportunity for the local population to look upon the project as its own."* For others, the Stadium is *"an insult to the population which is not able to get a basic living"*, *"an empty space most of the time, in an overcrowded suburb."*

The rationale behind such a policy decision is that sport infrastructures, and football in particular, have a role to play in promoting social mix in precise localities. *"Placed in problem areas, these infrastructures do not have a direct effect on the life of the neighbourhood. It is a way to have people know about a place and visit a district where they would never otherwise go."* Around the Stadium of France during the 1998 World Cup, *"a new urban life developed, with exhibitions where people expressed their ethnic roots. As such, it had an effect on the identity and the recognition of the local identity as it is."* This development has then been assessed as *"a good example of partnership between the state, local authorities, the private sector, neighbourhood and sport organisations. At the end of the process, local people were proud of their Stadium."* Is this still the case one year later when security problems have arisen around the Stadium of France and when it cannot attract many shows due to the sheer costs involved?

The concept of *"appropriation"* is pertinent for analysing the success or failure to integrate urban projects. *"It is not a problem of form but a problem of content: an infrastructure project in one place does not have the same effects as in another. It depends on whether local people are able to consider the project as their own, after a process involving community participation, and taking into account social identity considerations."* The social acceptance of a project is the outcome of several participatory actions and can be considered as *"a strategic concept and a condition of success for sustainable urban development."*

The Impacts of Social Housing Provision

A comparative evaluation of different approaches aimed at solving shelter problems would contribute to promoting the social agenda of city management. *"The Dutch have tried a model of the mass production of social housing. This approach was only feasible under very specific circumstances, as prevailed for decades in the Netherlands. In developing countries, however, the model is frequently one of self-help and of informal housing."* In the US, a new model of housing for the poor is now being put in place in large east-coast cities, whereby simple dwellings are being built in the owner-occupier sector, with private rental units attached to it. A model of cheap housing has also been tried in Cape Town (see Chapter 4.3). *"There is a need to focus on "good or feasible" practise in solving housing problems in different circumstances, taking for example New York, Cape Town and Rotterdam as different models. To define what works and under which circumstances."*

The Social Impacts of Transport

The role of transport infrastructures for the social development of cities also needs to be better highlighted in research. Clearly, *"transport underpins many other areas of urban management. Still, there is for example little understanding of the housing and transport linkages."* The social impact of transport is well illustrated in Cape Town, where the relocation of low-income people in the periphery has had negative consequences on metropolitan finance, as local authorities have had to allocate more social benefits.

In the past, planners have not adequately considered mobility as an urban and social value. *"Environmental sustainability has been placed as a priority, while mobility is central for social equity. There is a strong connection between the way people manage their own life, and mobility."* A central concern of policy-making and research has to be to explore the means and measures to integrate transport infrastructures with respect to both the environmental and social surroundings of urban areas.

Strengthening Social and Economic Linkages

In considerations about social sustainability, *"social and economic linkages are at present only vaguely discussed and need to be strengthened."* The way municipal councils are structured makes it easy to pay for visible products such as physical infrastructures or spatial plans. *"The question is how can a socially driven process of discussion, debate and participation, which leads to different forms of decision-making, be financed."*

In cities like Cape Town, the money that would be required for social processes is so great that the question remains unanswered. Elements of a response start to be given elsewhere — for example, the recent commitment of some Brazilian cities to provide finance for the social processes that lead to upgrading informal settlements (see Chapter 5. 5); the budget allocated in Milan for dealing with crime (see Chapter 3. 4); or the experiment in Lyon to utilise a people's budget process (see Chapter 2. 5). Long-term commitment for this type of initiative is just as important. *"Budgets are not only necessary to begin processes: implementation and follow-up budgets are as crucial."*

DEFINING A MODEL FOR SOCIALLY SUSTAINABLE URBAN DEVELOPMENT

Common Key Principles

Many cities in the MOST Network are committed to meet the challenge of socially sustainable urban development on the basis of a *three-fold approach*:

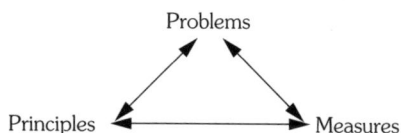

Urban policy is being initiated to address the following basic *problems*: economic development, urban integration, metropolitan management, exclusion and unemployment reduction, and environmental improvement. However, the scope and magnitude of these problems are not the same in cities like Nairobi, Cape Town, Geneva and Toronto. Similarly, the *measures* undertaken and means devoted to these policy areas are not comparable.

In contrast, all the cities are asking similar key questions and are proposing common *principles* for policy objectives including:
- implementing a metropolitan governance to avoid fragmenting the city and creating split communities;
- preparing a social agenda that favours social equity and cultural diversity, while avoiding spatial and social segregation;
- integrating transportation with land-use and neighbourhood life in order to favour urban integration;
- creating a culture of co-operation and partnership between the various urban stakeholders, at all geographical levels, from neighbourhoods to the metropolitan area.

For each of these objectives, a similar methodological approach is used which includes the following stages:
- presenting the central issues in their historical, social and geographical context;
- putting the issues in perspective within the present urban environment and its social and cultural values;
- defining priorities, planning objectives, and implementing planning measures;
- devoting the means to reach these objectives, often within a public-private sector partnership and co-operation;
- evaluating the results in quantitative and qualitative terms, over the short-, middle- and long-term.

Towards a Model

To bring together the different thematic approaches, new integrated policy models need to be defined for urban management. A prospective and integrated approach to metropolitan management is outlined below. This analysis links together visions of cities considered as:
- a physical and biological environment;
- a built environment;
- a social environment.

The integrative model is structured around five main principles:
- the economic principle of *"strengthening local potentials"*: to revive, to invest, to attract, to innovate, to create, to maintain;
- the social principle of *"social diversity and equity"*: social redistribution, spatial redistribution, cultural diversity;
- the ecological principle of *"environmental protection"*: the precautionary principle, balanced ecosystems;
- the geographical principle of *"spatial equity"*: metropolitan level governance, urban integration, minimised spatial disparities, fragmentation and exclusion avoidance;
- the political principle of *"autonomous urban management"*: governance based on democracy, endogenous and bottom-up decision-making, autonomy, subsidiarity, co-operation, partnership.

To develop the sustainability of cities, consideration must be given to the three types of urban environment mentioned above, and a balance must be achieved between the five main principles identified. *"This way of thinking about urban management gives greater importance to the urban stakeholder. The approach is to look at urban perceptions, to understand spatial systems and land-use."*

The urban challenges that local authorities face are: devising and implementing public policies to manage basic services and urban networks; promoting economic attractiveness; dealing with social disparities and spatial exclusion; and working for a better quality of life.

Such a city model is structured, according the experiences in the MOST Network, around the following objectives:
- implementating an integrated metropolitan governance;
- defining social projects and providing housing;

- struggling against crime;
- integrating transport and spatial planning;
- promoting an endogenous economic development.

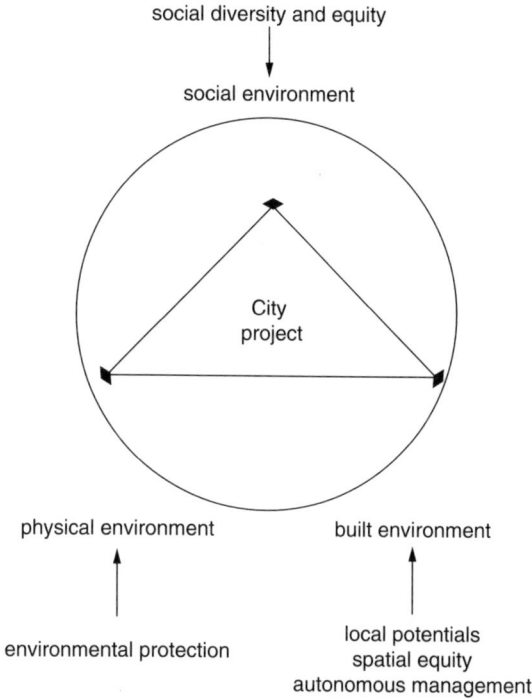

Linking the spatial and social dimensions of urban planning is central to promoting socially sustainable development in cities. This approach is a challenge. The complexity of the processes involved, the multiplicity of stakeholders, the various levels of possible action, make it clear that the only way forward is through a multi-disciplinary approach bringing together the many different visions and experiences in defining urban planning policies and programmes. The MOST Network on Socially Sustainable Cities has a strong potential to contribute to this goal in the future.

BIBLIOGRAPHY

Books

Anselme, M. (2000) *Du bruit à la parole, La scène politique des cités.* La Tour d'Aigues: Éditions de l'Aube.

Ascher, F. (1995) *Métapolis ou l'avenir des villes.* Paris: Odile Jacob.

Ashton, J. (ed.) (1992) *Healthy Cities.* Milton Keynes: Open University Press

Atkinson, G. et al. (eds) (1997) *Measuring Sustainable Development.* Cheltenham: Edward Elgar.

Bachmann, C. and Leguennec N. (1996) *Violences urbaines.* Paris: Albin Michel.

Bailly A. (ed.) (1997) *Terres d'exclusions, Terres d'espérances.* Paris: Economica.

Bailly, A. (1994) *"Territoires et territorialité."* In *Encyclopédie d'économie spatiale,* edited by J.P. Auray et al. Paris: Economica.

Bairoch, P. (1988) *Cities and Economic Development: From the dawn of history to the present.* London: Mansell (Original French edition, 1987, *De Jéricho à Mexico: villes et économie dans l'histoire.* Paris: Gallimard).

Barou, J. (1992) *La place du pauvre: Histoire et géographie sociale de l'habitat HLM.* Paris: L'Harmattan.

Baudrillard, J. et al. (1991) *Citoyenneté et urbanité.* Paris: Esprit.

Benyahoun, G., Gaussier, N., Planque, B. (eds.) (1999) *L'encrage territorial du développement durable: de nouvelles perspectives.* Paris/Montréal: L'Harmattan.

Burgess, R.E., Park, E.W. and McKenzie, R. (1925) *The City, Chicago.* Chicago: University of Chicago Press.

Burridge, R. and Ormandy, D. (eds.) (1993) *Unhealthy Housing: Research, Remedies and Reform.* London: E. and F.N. Spon.

Castells, M. (1989) *The Informational City: Information, Technology, Economic Restructuring and the Urban-Regional Process.* London: Basil Blackwell.

Castells, M. (1993) *The City and the Grassroots.* Berkeley and Los Angeles: University of California Press.

Dickens, P. (1992) *Society and Nature: Towards a green social theory.* London: Harvester Wheatsheaf.

Dommen, E. (1993) *Fair Principles for Sustainable Development: Essays on environmental policy and developing countries.* Aldershot UK: Edward Elgar.

Dubet, F. and Lapeyronnie, D. (1992) *Les quartiers d'exil.* Paris: Seuil.

Ellin, N. (1996) *Postmodern Urbanism.* Oxford: Blackwell.

Fainstein, S. and Hirst, C. (1995), *"Urban Social Movements."* In *Theories of Urban Politics,* edited by D. Judge, G. Stoker and H. Wolman. London: Thousand Oaks, New Delhi: Sage.

Faudry, D. (1993) *Génie urbain et urbanisme.* Lyon: INGUL.

Friedmann, J. (1987) *Planning in the Public Domain: From Knowledge to Action. Princeton,* NJ: Princeton University Press.

Garreau, J. (1991) *Edge Cities.* New York: Doubleday.

Hake, A. (1977) *African Metropolis.* Brighton: Sussex University Press.

Hall, P. (1998) Cities of Tomorrow: *An intellectual history of urban planning and design in the twentieth century.* Oxford: Basil Blackwell.

Hannerz, U. (1992) *Cultural Complexity: Studies in the social organization of meaning.* New York: Columbia University Press

Hardin, G. (1993) *Living Within Limits: Ecology, Economics and Population Taboos.* New York: Oxford University Press.

Herbert, D. T. and Johnson, R.J. (eds.) (1976) *Social Areas in Cities: Spatial Processes and Forms.* New York: Wiley.

Hohenberg, P. and Hollen Lees, L. (1995) *The Making of Urban Europe 1000-1994.* Cambridge, Mass.: Harvard University Press.

Huttman, E. (ed.) (1991) *Urban Housing Segregation of Minorities in Western Europe and the United States.* Durham and London: Duke University Press.

Jacobs, J. (1961) *Death and Life of Great American Cities.* New York: Random House.

Jelin, E. and Hersberg, E. (1996) *Constructing Democracy.* Boulder: Westview.

Judge, D., Stoker, G. and Wolman, H. (eds.) (1995) *Theories of Urban Politics.* London: Thousand Oaks, New Delhi: Sage.

Langdon, P. (1994) *A Better Place to Live: Reshaping the American Suburb. Amherst,* Mass: Massachusetts University Press.

Lawrence, R. (1995) *"Meeting the Challenge: Barriers to integrated cross-sectoral urban policies." In Urban Policies for an Environmentally Sustainable World,* edited by M. Rolén. Stockholm: Swedish Council for Planning and Co-ordination of Research.

Lawrence, R. (1996) *"Urban Environment, Health and the Economy: Cues for conceptual clarification and more effective policy implementation." In Our Cities, Our Future: Policies and Action Plans for Health and Sustainable Development.* Copenhagen: World Health Organisation/ OECD.

Lefebvre, H. (1968) *Le droit à la ville.* Paris: Anthropos.

Lofland, L.H. (1973) *A World of Strangers: Order and Action in Urban Public Spaces.* New York: Basic Books.

McCarney, P., Halfani M., and Rodriguez A. (1995) *"Towards an Understanding of Governance: The Emergence of an Idea and its Implications for Urban Research in Developing Countries." In Urban Research in the Developing World: Vol. 4, Perspectives on the City,* edited by R. Stren and J. Kjellberg Bell. Toronto: Centre for Urban and Community Studies, University of Toronto.

Maser, C., Beaton, R., and Smith, K. (eds.) (1998) *Setting the Stage for Sustainability.* Boca Raton: Lewis.

Musterd, S., Ostendorf, W., and Breebaart M. (1998) *Multi-Ethnic metropolis: Patterns and Policies.* Dordrecht: Kluwer.

O'Loughlin, J. and Friedrichs, J. (eds.) (1996) *Social Polarization in Post-Industrial Metropolises.* Berlin/New York: De Gruyter.

Palne Kovacs Ilona (2000) *Regionalis politika es kozigazgatas. (Regional policy and Public Administration)* Pecs: Dialog Campus.

Petonnet, C. (1982) *Espaces habités, ethnologie des banlieues.* Paris: Galilée.

Polèse, M. and Stren, R. (eds.) (2000) *The Social Sustainability of Cities: Diversity and the Management of Change.* Toronto: University of Toronto Press.

Rao, P. K. (1999) Sustainable Development, Economics and Policy. Blackwell: Malden.

Ravetz, A. (1980) *Remaking Cities: Contradictions of the Recent Urban Environment,* London: Croom Helm.

Ravetz, A. (1986) *The Government of Space: Town Planning in Modern Society.* London: Faber and Faber.

Reid, D. 1995. *Sustainable Development: An introductory guide.* London: Earthscan.

Robson, B. (1988) *Those Inner Cities: Reconciling the economic and social aims of urban policy.* Oxford: Clarendon Press.

Rolén, M. (ed.) (1995) *Urban Policies for an Environmentally Sustainable World.* Stockholm: Swedish Council for Planning and Co-ordination of Research.

Rusk, D. (1993) *Cities without Suburbs.* Washington DC: Woodrow Wilson Center Press.

Sachs, I. (1993) *Transition Strategies Towards the 21st century.* New-Delhi: Interest Publications.

Sachs-Jeantet, C. (1994) *Humaniser la ville. Les enjeux de la citoyenneté et de l'urbanité.* Paris: Independent Commission for Population and Quality of Life, UNESCO.

Stren, R. et al. (1992) An Urban Problematique: *The Challenge of Urbanization for Development Assistance.* Toronto: Centre for Urban and Community Studies, University of Toronto.

Stren, R., Halfani M. and Malombe J. (1994) *"Coping with Urbanization and Urban Policy." In Beyond Capitalism vs. Socialism in Kenya and Tanzania,* edited by Joel D. Barkan. Boulder, Colorado: Lynne Reiner.

Vance, J. E. Jr. (1976) *"Institutional Forces that Shape the City."* In *Social Areas in Cities: Spatial Processes and Forms,* edited by D. T. Herbert and R.J Johnson. New York: Wiley.

Viellard-Baron, H. (1997) *"Les banlieues françaises entre exclusion et intégration."* In *Terres d'exclusions, Terres d'espérances,* edited by A. Bailly. Paris: Economica.

Weiher, G. (1991) *The Fragmented Metropolis.* Albany: State University of New York Press.

Williams, S. (1994) *Environment and Mental Health.* New York: John Wiley.

Wilson, W.J. (1987) *The Truly Disadvantaged. The Inner City, The Underclass, and Public Policy.* Chicago: University of Chicago Press.

World Commission on Environment and Development (1987) *Our Common Future (The Bruntland Report).* New York: Oxford University Press.

JOURNALS

Arnstein, S. (1969) *"A ladder of citizen participation",* Journal of the American Institute of Planners 35, 4.

Ascher F. (1991) *"Les principes du nouvel urbanisme."* Sociedade e Territorio 13, 119-126.

Bolt, G., Burgers, J. and Van Kempen, R. (1998) *"On the social significance of spatial location: spatial segregation and social inclusion."* Netherlands Journal of Housing and the Built Environment 13(1), 83-95.

Callon, M. (1996) *"Le travail de la conception en architecture."* Cahiers de la recherche architecturale 37, 25-35.

Collective. (1992) *"Banlieues: relégation ou citoyenneté."* Les Temps modernes 545-546 (Jan.) Paris.

Collective. (1997) *"Professionnaliser la médiation sociale – Pour un statut des femmes relais."* Profession Banlieue (Dec.).

Collective. (1997) *"Santiago Lyon Montréal: partenaires pour le développement urbain."* Economie et humanisme 346 (Nov.), Lyon.

Collective (Journal). (1998) *"Action sociale et politique de la ville: vers une refondation du droit commun ?"* Les Cahiers du CR.DSU 19 (June), Lyon.

Collective. (1999) *"Quand la ville se défait ?" (De la question sociale à la question territoriale. L'avenir de la ville. Peut-on parler de sécession urbaine? États-Unis Amérique latine, Europe).* Esprit 258 (November).

Harris, C. D. and Ullman E. L. *(1945) "The Nature of Cities." Annals of the American Academy of Political and Social Science CCXLII, 7-17.*

Jacobs, J. M, (1993) *"The City Unbound: qualitative approaches to the city."* Urban Studies 30 (4-5), 827-848.

Lawrence, R. (1999) *"Urban Health: an Ecological Perspective."* Reviews on Environmental Health 14, 1, 1-10.

Werlin H. (1999) *"The Slum Upgrading Myth."* Urban Studies 39,9, 1523-1535.

REPORTS

Commission of the European Communities (1993) *Towards Sustainability. The European Commission's Progress Report and Action Plan on the 5th Programme of Policy and Action in Relation to the Environment and Sustainable Development.* Luxembourg: Office of Official Publications.

Commission of the European Communities (1997) *Towards an Urban Agenda in the European Union.* Brussels: Communication from the Commission, COM(97)197 final.

Delarue, J.-M. (1991) *Banlieues en difficultés: La relégation.* Paris: Syros/Alternatives.

Jacquier, C. (1993) *Quartiers en crise: laboratoires de la citoyenneté européenne? Programme 1991-1993: rapport final.* Bruxelles: OCDE Commission européenne.

Organisation for Economic Co-operation and Development (OECD) (1990) *Cities and New Technologies. Paris: OECD.*

OECD (1991) *Environmental Policies for Cities in the 1990s.* Paris: OECD.

OECD (1994) *The multisectoral approach to urban regeneration: Towards a new strategy for social integration, housing affordability and livable environments.* Paris: OECD.

OECD (1995) *Urban Travel and Sustainable Development.* Paris: OECD.

OECD (1996) *Strategies for Housing and Social Integration in Cities.* Paris: OECD.

OECD (1996) *Innovative Policies for Sustainable Urban Development: The Ecological City.* Paris: OECD.

OECD, (1997) *Better Understanding Our Cities: The role of urban indicators.* Paris: OECD.

OECD, (1988) *Integrating Distressed Urban Areas.* Paris: OECD.

Sueur, J.P. (1998) *Demain la ville. Tome 1 et tome 2.* Paris: Documentation française.

UNCHS-Habitat (1986) *Global Report on Human Settlements.* Oxford: Oxford University Press.

UNCHS-Habitat (1996) *An Urbanising World.* Oxford: Oxford University Press.

UNDP (1991) *Cities, People and Poverty. Urban Development Cooperation for the 1990s.* New York: UNDP.

World Health Organisation (WHO) (1996) *Our Cities, Our Future: Policies and action plans for health and sustainable development.* Copenhagen: WHO.

WHO (1997) *Sustainable Development and Health: Concepts, principles and framework for action for European cities and towns.* Copenhagen: WHO.

WHO (1997) *City Planning for Health and Sustainable Development.* Copenhagen: WHO.

WWW. LINKS

Blakely, E., Fallon, M. and Hoffman, S. (1995) *"Social Equity in Planning." California Planning Roundtable,* Los Angeles. http://www.cmcaplans.com/cprwww/docs/equity (15 June)

Krumholtz, N. and Forester, J. (1990) *"Making Equity Planning Work; Leadership in the Public Sector."* Cleveland Policy Planning Report, Cleveland. Quoted in Blakely, E., Fallon, M. and Hoffman, S. (1995) http://www.cmcaplans.com/cprwww/docs/equity (15 June)

OECD, *Sustainable Development.* http://www.oecd.org/subject/sustdev

UNESCO, MOST Theme 2: *Cities as arenas of social transformations.* http://www.unesco.org/most/most2.htm

UNESCO, MOST Policy Development — Socially Sustainable Cities. http://www.unesco.org/most/p3soc.htm

van Wensveen F. W. (1999) The Rotterdam Virtual Tour,

http://www.euronet.nl/users/frankvw/rotterdam.html (1 November).

United Nations Centre for Human Settlements (Habitat), *The Together Foundation (1996-1999),* Best Practices Local Leadership Programme (BLP). http://www.bestpractices.org

United Nations Centre for Human Settlements (Habitat), The Together Foundation (1996-1999), *Urban Management Programme.* http://www.urbanobservatory.org/unchs

WHO, Centre for Urban Health: *Healthy Cities Project.* http://www.who.dk/healthy-cities

CAPE TOWN CONFERENCE PAPERS 1998

Abbott, J. *Servicing Informal Settlements: A Case Study From South Africa*

Bailly, A. S. *Large Transport Infrastructures and Quality of Life*

Beiser, M. *Language Acquisition, Employment and Mental Health among Southeast Asian Refugees: A Ten-Year Study*

Bourne, L.S. *Migration, Immigration and Social Sustainability: The Recent Toronto Experience*

Cardia, C. *Vitality and Safety, a Projection for the Milan Urban Fringe*

Dieleman, F. M. *Can Housing Policy Help to Create Socially Sustainable Cities?*

Dubois-Taine, G. *About New Urban Values*

Enyedi, G. *Governing Metropolitan Budapest*

Fisher, S. *Integrated Development Planning in the Cape Metropolitan Area*

Germain, A. *Living with Cultural and Ethnic Diversity: An Urban Affair – the Case of Montreal*

Keresztély, K. *Evolution of the Metropolitan Government in Budapest*

Lawrence, R. J. *Qualities of Urban Habitats and Socially Sustainable Development: Key Issues from a Survey in Canton Geneva*

Lee-Smith, D. and Lamba, D.

Social Transformation in a Post-Colonial City: The Case of Nairobi

Lungo, M. *Metropolitan Planning and Civil Society Participation in Developing Urban Governance Relations in El Salvador*

Ongjerth, R. *Governing and Planning Issues of Budapest Region: The M0 Motorway around Budapest*

Pal-Kovacs, I.   *The Dilemmas of Metropolitan Governance by the Example of Budapest*

Saule, N. Jr.   *Housing Policy Management Systems: Brazilian Experiences*

Voisin, B.   *Social Development and Local Governance in Greater Lyon*

Impression : EUROPE MEDIA DUPLICATION S.A.
53110 Lassay-les-Châteaux
N° 8063 - Dépôt légal : décembre 2000